Entertaining
for the Holidays

Jean Paré

www.companyscoming.com
visit our  website

Front Cover

1. Smoked Salmon Triangles, page 21

Back Cover

1. Holiday Gingerbread Bundt, page 134
2. Peppermint Mini-Cupcakes, page 131

Props: HomeSense

Entertaining For The Holidays

Copyright © Company's Coming Publishing Limited

First Printing October 2011

Library and Archives Canada Cataloguing in Publication
Paré, Jean, date-
Entertaining for the holidays / Jean Paré.
(Original series) Includes index.
At head of title: Company's Coming.
ISBN 978-1-897477-45-8
1. Holiday cookery. 2. Entertaining. I. Title. II.
Series: Paré, Jean, date. Original series.
TX739.P36 2010   641.5'68   C2010-900563-5

Published by
Company's Coming Publishing Limited
2311 – 96 Street
Edmonton, Alberta, Canada T6N 1G3
Tel: 780-450-6223   Fax: 780-450-1857
www.companyscoming.com

Company's Coming is a registered trademark owned by Company's Coming Publishing Limited

We acknowledge the financial support of the Government of Canada through the Canada Book Fund for our publishing activities.

Printed in China

We gratefully acknowledge the following suppliers for their generous support of our Test and Photography Kitchens:

Broil King Barbecues
Corelle®
Hamilton Beach® Canada
Lagostina®
Proctor Silex® Canada
Tupperware®

Our special thanks to the following business for providing props for photography:

Le Gnome

Table of Contents

Appetizers & Snacks

Breads

Salads & Soups

Beef

Pork & Lamb

Vegetarian

Candies & Cookies

Desserts

The Company's Coming Story

Jean Paré (pronounced "jeen PAIR-ee") grew up understanding that the combination of family, friends and home cooking is the best recipe for a good life. From her mother, she learned to appreciate good cooking, while her father praised even her earliest attempts in the kitchen. When Jean left home, she took with her a love of cooking, many family recipes and an intriguing desire to read cookbooks as if they were novels!

"Never share a recipe you wouldn't use yourself."

When her four children had all reached school age, Jean volunteered to cater the 50th anniversary celebration of the Vermilion School of Agriculture, now Lakeland College, in Alberta, Canada. Working out of her home, Jean prepared a dinner for more than 1,000 people, launching a flourishing catering operation that continued for over 18 years. During that time, she had countless opportunities to test new ideas with immediate feedback—resulting in empty plates and contented customers! Whether preparing cocktail sandwiches for a house party or serving a hot meal for 1,500 people, Jean Paré earned a reputation for great food, courteous service and reasonable prices.

As requests for her recipes increased, Jean was often asked the question, "Why don't you write a cookbook?" Jean responded by teaming up with her son, Grant Lovig, in the fall of 1980 to form Company's Coming Publishing Limited. The publication of *150 Delicious Squares* on April 14, 1981 marked the debut of what would soon become one of the world's most popular cookbook series.

The company has grown since those early days when Jean worked from a spare bedroom in her home. Today, she continues to write recipes while working closely with the staff of the Recipe Factory, as the Company's Coming test kitchen is affectionately known.

There she fills the role of mentor, assisting with the development of recipes people most want to use for everyday cooking and easy entertaining. Every Company's Coming recipe is *kitchen-tested* before it is approved for publication.

Jean's daughter, Gail Lovig, is responsible for marketing and distribution, leading a team that includes sales personnel located in major cities across Canada. Company's Coming cookbooks are distributed in Canada, the United States, Australia and other world markets. Bestsellers many times over in English, Company's Coming cookbooks have also been published in French and Spanish.

Familiar and trusted in home kitchens around the world, Company's Coming cookbooks are offered in a variety of formats. Highly regarded as kitchen workbooks, the softcover Original Series, with its lay-flat plastic comb binding, is still a favourite among readers.

Jean Paré's approach to cooking has always called for *quick and easy recipes* using *everyday ingredients.* That view has served her well. The recipient of many awards, including the Queen Elizabeth Golden Jubilee Medal, Jean was appointed Member of the Order of Canada, her country's highest lifetime achievement honour.

Jean continues to gain new supporters by adhering to what she calls The Golden Rule of Cooking: *Never share a recipe you wouldn't use yourself.* It's an approach that has worked—*millions of times over!*

Foreword

The jewel-toned colours, sparkle, music and traditions of the holiday season make it a magical time of year. Part of the experience is catching up with friends and family and sharing recipes that we pull out only at Christmas or New Year's. This year, make *Entertaining for the Holidays* a part of your holiday traditions. This all-new collection of delicious recipes includes a wide range of traditional favourites as well as some new ones that you will want to add to your repertoire year after year.

No matter what style of entertaining you plan to do, you'll find something in *Entertaining for the Holidays* to suit any occasion or taste. Try our Stuffed Yorkshire Puddings and Wild Rice-Stuffed Turkey for a twist on tradition. Smoked Salmon Roll-Ups, Winter White Bean Dip, Cranberry Salsa Bites, Festive Eggnog and Toffee Truffle Brownies are perfect cocktail party fare. If you're on a diet or just want to avoid heavy holiday foods, we've covered that too. Turkey Romaine Spears, Chèvre Pear Quesadillas, Ginger Chops With Mandarin Salsa and Spanish Lentil Spinach Soup are among the many lighter recipes we've included. Do you enjoy making your own gifts? Delicious recipes like Vanilla Chai Tea Liqueur, Ginger Quick Bread or Chocolate Peanut Bark will let you give your gifts a personal touch.

We know the holidays can be hectic, so to help you stay organized, we've included an assortment of recipes that are prepared the night before and others that can be frozen long in advance. We've also included recipes that can be put together quickly when you need to get dinner ready in a hurry. Some recipes have been designed to produce many servings, or are easy to double, for those times when you're expecting a crowd. A range of beverages is also provided, including alcohol-free drinks to help make sure guests get home safely.

Take a breath, relax and let *Entertaining for the Holidays* carry you merrily through the holidays!

Jean Paré

Nutrition Information Guidelines

Each recipe is analyzed using the most current version of the Canadian Nutrient File from Health Canada, which is based on the United States Department of Agriculture (USDA) Nutrient Database.

- If more than one ingredient is listed (such as "butter or hard margarine"), or if a range is given (1 – 2 tsp., 5 – 10 mL), only the first ingredient or first amount is analyzed.

- For meat, poultry and fish, the serving size per person is based on the recommended 4 oz. (113 g) uncooked weight (without bone), which is 2 – 3 oz. (57 – 85 g) cooked weight (without bone)—approximately the size of a deck of playing cards.

- Milk used is 1% M.F. (milk fat), unless otherwise stated.

- Cooking oil used is canola oil, unless otherwise stated.

- Ingredients indicating "sprinkle," "optional," or "for garnish" are not included in the nutrition information.

- The fat in recipes and combination foods can vary greatly depending on the sources and types of fats used in each specific ingredient. For these reasons, the amount of saturated, monounsaturated and polyunsaturated fats may not add up to the total fat content.

Vera C. Mazurak, Ph.D.
Nutritionist

5

Here Come the Holidays!

The days leading up to Christmas through to New Year's Day are some of the busiest and most festive of the year. It's also the time when we tend to do more entertaining, and on a much larger scale, than at any other time of the year. Familiar holiday songs surround us as we brave the hustle and bustle of the shops, searching for the perfect gifts. Trimming the tree, planning parties, attending Christmas concerts and writing cards are all part of what makes the season so special.

Of course, the season would not be complete without lots of great food. Since the holidays can sometimes leave you tired and frazzled, it's important to plan ahead and keep the preparations as simple as possible. To help, we've included some time-saving tips for hosting great get-togethers without missing out on the fun!

Planning Your Gathering

Before planning any get-together, you'll need to decide how much time and money to budget, who to invite and the style of entertaining that best fits.

Budgeting Time and Money

Consider your schedule and your budget, particularly if you will be hosting more than one occasion. The last thing you want is to plan parties so elaborate that you spend every waking moment planning them, or break the bank buying supplies! Set a budget that is realistic. Try to plan menus with everyday ingredients and choose seasonal produce that is more likely to be readily available and reasonably priced. You can avoid additional stress by making as much food as possible in advance. Don't be afraid to purchase a few pre-made or convenience products that will help to simplify your menu or save you a little time.

Make Ahead

To take some of the stress out of hosting, many recipes can be made a few days ahead and chilled until ready to serve, or frozen a month or two in advance.

Most of our recipes for cakes, squares, cookies and candies can be made ahead and stored in the freezer for up to two months, allowing you to plan and prepare treats well in advance of the busy holiday season. This also allows you to keep some sweets on hand for those times that unexpected guests drop in.

Invite List

When planning your guest list, consider how many people will comfortably fit into your space. Instead of hosting one large party, consider hosting a few smaller ones. Smaller parties are easier to organize, plan and put on, and they create a more intimate atmosphere, which both you and your guests might prefer. If your guests aren't already familiar with one another, it might be good to consider how those on your guest list might mix and mingle.

Style of Entertaining

The style of entertaining that best fits your event depends upon several factors—the type of food you plan to serve, the theme of the event (if you have one), the size of the guest list, and whether the event is to be casual or formal are all important considerations.

Most parties fall into one of three broad categories:

Buffets	• Perfect for casual entertaining—because guests serve themselves, you'll have more time to mingle. • Buffets lend themselves well to potluck-style entertaining. • Buffets can also work well as a single-course event, such as a dessert buffet.
Sit-Down Meals	• Sit-down meals are more intimate and can be either casual or formal. • For a formal affair, plate the food yourself as you serve it. • For a more casual sit-down meal, bring bowls and platters to the table so people can serve themselves. • This style of entertaining has the advantage of having guests at one table, allowing everyone to join the conversation.
Cocktail Parties	• Cocktail parties offer a great deal of flexibility in what you can select to serve—both appetizers and desserts work exceptionally well. • Because people usually move around at these kinds of parties, there's no need to set a table, but you may wish to have a few food and drink stations set up to encourage mingling. • At cocktail parties, the beverages are often just as important as the food. • This type of party also works well as a potluck.

Menu Planning for Success

The next step in planning your gathering is setting your menu. There are a few considerations you will need to take into account when embarking upon this task.

If you are hosting Christmas or New Year's dinner, you may choose to go with a more traditional meal. Or, if you're hosting a potluck, you may want to request that guests bring a certain type of dish so that all the bases are covered. Perhaps you don't wish to host a meal at all, but rather a cookie exchange or a dessert buffet?

It's always important to consider whether the dishes you've chosen can be prepared in unison, using either similar cooking methods or oven temperatures, or select at least a few recipes that can be made in advance and reheated. If you're hosting a casual meal on a weeknight, selecting dishes that make the best use of your time will be important, so choose those that can be made in a flash or even a few that make use of your slow cooker!

For any menu, don't forget to consider your guests' dietary restrictions or taste preferences, and be sure to offer a few healthier options. We've also included several recipes inspired by the holiday traditions of other cultures, such as Roasted Borscht (page 58), Potato Parsnip Latkes (page 106) and a Panettone Braid (page 32).

What Will You Serve?

To give you some ideas of how you can mix and match the recipes in this book to create interesting and balanced party menus, here are some sample menus to fit a few different occasions:

Family Brunch for 4 to 6

Main Course:	Berry French Toast Sandwiches (page 47) or
	Cranberry Orange Blintzes (page 48)
	Cooked sausages or bacon
Side Dish:	Festive Fruit Medley (page 49)
Dessert:	Cardamom Hot Chocolate (page 24)
	Toffee Truffle Brownies (page 138)

Holiday Party Buffet for 8 to 10 (or more)

Appetizers:	Mushroom Lentil Tapenade (page 19) with toasted baguette
	Smoked Salmon Triangles (page 21)
Main Courses:	Fig and Apple-Stuffed Pork (page 78)
	Honey Cajun Salmon (page 73)
Vegetarian Main Course or Side Dish:	Curry Vegetable Pilaf (page 97)
Side Dishes:	Fennel Potato Gratin (page 110)
	Maple Mustard Green Beans x 2 (page 105)
Salad:	Cranberry Confetti Slaw (page 52)
Desserts:	Chocolate Mole Fondue (page 151) with fresh fruit
	Cookie Tray with: Cranberry Pistachio Cookies (page 130)
	Chocolate Spice Cookies (page 123)
	White Chocolate Panforte (page 117)

Casual Sit-Down Social for 6 to 8

Main Course:	Tuscan Winter Stew x 2 (page 96) or
	Take-the-Chill-Off Chili (page 64)
Bread:	Savoury Herb Biscuits (page 34)
Side Dish:	Roasted Broccoli and Brussels (page 116)
Salad:	Parmesan Pear Salad (page 59)
Dessert:	Fruity Rice Pudding (page 149)

Low-Stress Weeknight Dinner for 6 to 8

Appetizer:	Winter White Bean Dip (page 20) with veggies and crackers
Main Course:	Cranberry Pot Roast (page 61)
Side Dish:	Creamy Roasted Garlic Potatoes (page 112)
Bread:	Overnight Dinner Rolls (page 38)
Salad:	Cranberry Confetti Slaw (page 52)
Dessert:	An assortment of cookies and squares from your freezer

Christmas Cookie Exchange

Chocolate Spice Cookies (page 123)
White Chocolate Cherry Cookies (page 118)
Cranberry Pistachio Cookies (page 130)
Fruit and Cashew Clusters (page 127)

Food and Beverage Portions

Our recipes provide a good estimate of portion sizes, but you may find the following information useful in determining how much food and drink you might require.

Beverages

Exactly what constitues a drink? Below, we've provided some standard serving sizes for alcoholic beverages. Remember to provide an assortment of non-alcoholic beverages as well, including tea and coffee.

Type of Beverage	Standard Serving Size
Beer	12 oz. (341 mL)
Wine or Champagne	5 oz. (142 mL)
Liqueurs	1 oz. (30 mL)
Spirits	1 1/2 oz. (45 mL) Note: For every 26 oz. (750 mL) bottle of spirits, you should provide approximately 3 similarly sized bottles of mix.

Food

Not sure how much food to budget per guest? The following is an example of how much a typical person might eat at a holiday feast.

Type of Course	Amount Per Person
Appetizers (finger food)	3 to 4 pieces at a sit-down meal 10 to 12 pieces at an appetizer party
Cheese	1 to 2 oz. (28 to 57 g) at a sit-down meal 3 to 4 oz. (85 to 113 g) at an appetizer party
Salads	1 cup (250 mL) leafy greens
Meat	3 to 5 oz. (85 to 140 g) cooked weight
Fish & Shellfish	5 oz. (140 g) cooked weight
Pasta, Rice or Potatoes	1/2 to 1 cup (125 to 250 mL)
Vegetables	1/2 cup (125 mL) of each vegetable dish
Cake or Pie	1/8 of a 9 inch (23 cm) pie or cake
Squares	3 to 4 pieces

Comforting Kitchen Gifts

Among the most thoughtful gifts are those you make yourself—especially those made in your kitchen! Many recipes in *Entertaining for the Holidays* make ideal gifts and are sure to be well-received. Remember to include any storage directions. You can do this by writing them on the back of an attached greeting tag.

Try pairing Chili Pecans (page 20) with a new DVD for the movie buff on your list. Or treat your favourite bookworm to Cranberry Pistachio Cookies (page 130) or Gingerbread Biscotti (page 124) with a popular book from the Bestsellers List. You can even spread the holiday cheer by giving a bottle of Holiday Cran-Apple Schnapps (page 25).

Keep in mind that gift containers can be functional too. Find festively coloured, airtight storage containers to hold your goodies, and not only will the treats stay fresh—the recipient will have a useful container that they can keep.

A Final Note About Holiday Entertaining

In the busy days ahead, don't forget to take a break from the rush and relax. Above all, remember that the primary reason for entertaining is to enjoy the company of family and friends at this wonderful time of year.

Crab and Fennel Spread

It just wouldn't be a party without a great dip! Serve this mild and cheesy crab spread with your favourite dippers like bell pepper pieces, crackers, cucumber slices and tortilla chips.

Lemon juice	2 tbsp.	30 mL
Cooking oil	1 tbsp.	15 mL
Fennel seed, crushed (see Note)	1/2 tsp.	2 mL
Salt	1/4 tsp.	1 mL
Pepper	1/4 tsp.	1 mL
Cans of crabmeat (6 oz., 170 g, each), drained, cartilage removed, flaked	2	2
Finely diced fennel bulb (white part only)	1 1/2 cups	375 mL
Block cream cheese, softened	8 oz.	250 g
Sour cream	1/2 cup	125 mL
Blue cheese dressing	1/4 cup	60 mL
Diced tomato, seeds removed	1 cup	250 mL
Sliced green onion	1/4 cup	60 mL

Combine first 5 ingredients in medium bowl.

Add crabmeat and fennel. Stir.

Combine next 3 ingredients in small bowl. Spread evenly on serving plate. Spoon crabmeat mixture over cream cheese mixture.

Scatter tomato and green onion over top. Makes about 5 1/2 cups (1.4 L).

1/4 cup (60 mL): 88 Calories; 7.1 g Total Fat (1.4 g Mono, 0.4 g Poly, 3.3 g Sat); 30 mg Cholesterol; 2 g Carbohydrate; trace Fibre; 4 g Protein; 129 mg Sodium

Note: To crush fennel seed, place in large resealable freezer bag. Seal bag. Gently hit with flat side of meat mallet or with rolling pin.

Stuffed Yorkshire Puddings

With a sprinkle of beef and horseradish, these puddings have a fun look and addictively savoury flavours! Leftover beef from Cranberry Pot Roast, page 61, can be used.

All-purpose flour	1 cup	250 mL
Salt	1/2 tsp.	2 mL
Pepper	1/4 tsp.	1 mL
Large eggs	3	3
Milk	1 cup	250 mL
Finely chopped deli sliced beef (or minced cooked roast beef)	1/3 cup	75 mL
Creamed horseradish	2 tbsp.	30 mL
Dijon mustard	1 tbsp.	15 mL
Finely chopped green onion	1 tbsp.	15 mL
Cooking oil	2 tbsp.	30 mL

Combine first 3 ingredients in medium bowl. Make a well in centre.

Beat eggs and milk in small bowl. Add to well. Beat until smooth. Let stand, covered, for 30 minutes.

Combine next 4 ingredients in separate small bowl.

Spoon 1/2 tsp. (2 mL) cooking oil into each of 12 muffin cups. Heat in 400°F (205°C) oven for about 5 minutes until oil is hot. Remove from oven. Stir milk mixture. Carefully fill muffin cups 1/3 full. Quickly spoon about 1 tsp. (5 mL) beef mixture over milk mixture in each muffin cup. Bake for about 25 minutes until puffed and golden. Makes 12 puddings.

1 pudding: 90 Calories; 3.9 g Total Fat (1.9 g Mono, 0.9 g Poly, 0.7 g Sat); 56 mg Cholesterol; 9 g Carbohydrate; trace Fibre; 4 g Protein; 197 mg Sodium

Paré Pointer
The day before Christmas, Adam said, "It's Christmas, Eve."

Cranberry Salsa Bites

Sweet cranberry salsa tops sharp goat cheese and baguette slices for a colourful and sophisticated New Year's Eve offering.

Frozen (or fresh) cranberries, thawed	1 1/2 cups	375 mL
Coarsely chopped orange	1/2 cup	125 mL
Liquid honey	2 tbsp.	30 mL
Coarsely chopped fresh jalapeño pepper (see Note)	1 tbsp.	15 mL
Frozen concentrated orange juice, thawed	1 tbsp.	15 mL
Coarsely chopped ginger root	1 tsp.	5 mL
Chopped fresh cilantro	1 1/2 tsp.	7 mL
Chopped fresh parsley	1 1/2 tsp.	7 mL
Grated orange zest	1/2 tsp.	2 mL
Baguette bread slices (1/2 inch, 12 mm, thick)	20	20
Cooking oil	2 tbsp.	30 mL
Goat (chèvre) cheese, softened	4 oz.	113 g

Process first 6 ingredients in food processor until finely chopped. Transfer to medium bowl.

Add next 3 ingredients. Stir.

Brush both sides of bread slices with cooking oil. Arrange on ungreased baking sheet. Broil on top rack in oven for about 1 minute per side until golden. Cool.

Spread cheese over toast slices. Top with cranberry mixture. Makes 20 bites.

1 bite: 65 Calories; 3.3 g Total Fat (1.2 g Mono, 0.5 g Poly, 1.3 g Sat); 5 mg Cholesterol; 7 g Carbohydrate; 5 g Fibre; 2 g Protein; 64 mg Sodium

Note: Hot peppers contain capsaicin in the seeds and ribs. Removing the seeds and ribs will reduce the heat. Wear rubber gloves when handling hot peppers and avoid touching your eyes. Wash your hands well afterwards.

Turkey Romaine Spears

Creamy turkey salad in crisp lettuce boats—an elegant hors d'oeuvre that's perfect for the health-conscious guest. You could use leftover turkey from Wild Rice-Stuffed Turkey, page 86. Try replacing the romaine with endive leaves for a slightly different taste and appearance.

Finely chopped cooked turkey	1 cup	250 mL
Chive and onion cream cheese	1/2 cup	125 mL
Diced unpeeled tart apple (such as Granny Smith)	1/2 cup	125 mL
Chopped green onion	2 tbsp.	30 mL
Finely chopped red pepper	2 tbsp.	30 mL
Romaine lettuce heart leaves	24	24

Combine first 5 ingredients in medium bowl.

Spoon onto lettuce leaves. Makes 24 spears.

1 spear: 50 Calories; 3.7 g Total Fat (0.1 g Mono, 0.1 g Poly, 2.4 g Sat); 14 mg Cholesterol; 1 g Carbohydrate; trace Fibre; 2 g Protein; 50 mg Sodium

Pictured on page 17.

Smoked Salmon Roll-Ups

Creamy smoked salmon and dill contrast with crunchy red onion and bean sprouts in these flavourful spirals. This lighter option doesn't sacrifice flavour and would be a welcomed addition to any buffet table!

Finely chopped smoked salmon (about 2 oz., 57 g)	1/4 cup	60 mL
Light cream cheese, softened	3 tbsp.	50 mL
Finely chopped red onion	2 tbsp.	30 mL
Chopped fresh dill (or 3/4 tsp., 4 mL, dried)	1 tbsp.	15 mL
Lime juice	2 tsp.	10 mL
Cajun seasoning	1/2 tsp.	2 mL
Pepper	1/8 tsp.	0.5 mL

(continued on next page)

Whole-wheat flour tortillas (10 inch, 25 cm, diameter)	2	2
Chopped fresh bean sprouts	1 cup	250 mL

Combine first 7 ingredients in small bowl.

Spread salmon mixture over each tortilla, almost to edge. Scatter bean sprouts over top. Roll up tightly, jelly-roll style. Trim ends. Cut each roll diagonally into 8 slices. Makes 16 roll-ups.

1 roll-up: 33 Calories; 0.8 g Total Fat (0.2 g Mono, 0.1 g Poly, 0.3 g Sat); 2 mg Cholesterol; 6 g Carbohydrate; 1 g Fibre; 2 g Protein; 96 mg Sodium

---

Cheese and Bacon Bites

These savoury shortbread bites have nippy cheese and smoky bacon that go perfectly with the Honey Mustard Dip. The bites can be made ahead and frozen in an airtight container for up to two months.

All-purpose flour	2 cups	500 mL
Grated sharp Cheddar cheese	1 cup	250 mL
Butter (or hard margarine), softened	3/4 cup	175 mL
Bacon slices, cooked crisp and crumbled	8	8
Worcestershire sauce	2 tsp.	10 mL
Dry mustard	1/2 tsp.	2 mL
Cayenne pepper	1/4 tsp.	1 mL
HONEY MUSTARD DIP		
Mayonnaise	1/2 cup	125 mL
Liquid honey	2 tbsp.	30 mL
Prepared mustard	2 tsp.	10 mL

Process first 7 ingredients in food processor with on/off motion until dough forms a ball. Roll into balls, using 1 tbsp. (15 mL) for each. Arrange in single layer on greased cookie sheets. Flatten with fork. Bake in 375°F (190°C) oven for about 15 minutes until firm and lightly browned. Remove from cookie sheets and place on wire racks to cool.

Honey Mustard Dip: Combine all 3 ingredients in small bowl. Makes about 2/3 cup (150 mL). Serve with bites. Makes about 38 bites.

1 bite with 1 tsp. (5 mL) dip: 89 Calories; 6.4 g Total Fat (2.8 g Mono, 0.7 g Poly, 3.1 g Sat); 14 mg Cholesterol; 6 g Carbohydrate; trace Fibre; 2 g Protein; 114 mg Sodium

Oven-Baked Brie

An attractive brie that can be served whole, warm from the oven with crackers. Enjoy the rich flavour of flaky pastry and sweet berry bites.

Package of puff pastry (14 oz., 397 g), thawed according to package directions	1/2	1/2
Brie cheese round	1 lb.	450 g
Dried blueberries	1/4 cup	60 mL
Dried cranberries	1/4 cup	60 mL
Egg yolk (large)	1	1
Water	1 tsp.	5 mL

Roll out puff pastry on lightly floured surface to 12 x 12 inch (30 x 30 cm) square. Trim corners at an angle. Cut decorative shapes from trimmings.

Cut cheese round in half horizontally. Place 1 half, cut-side up, in centre of pastry. Scatter blueberries and cranberries over cheese. Cover with remaining half, cut-side down. Fold edges of pastry together over cheese to enclose. Press edges to seal. Place, seam-side down, on greased baking sheet with sides.

Combine egg yolk and water in small bowl. Brush over pastry. Arrange decorative shapes over top. Brush with remaining egg yolk mixture. Cut 5 small vents in top to allow steam to escape. Bake on centre rack in 450°F (230°C) oven for about 15 minutes until pastry is golden brown. Let stand on baking sheet for 10 minutes. Serves 8.

1 serving: 325 Calories; 23.2 g Total Fat (4.8 g Mono, 0.6 g Poly, 11.9 g Sat); 83 mg Cholesterol; 15 g Carbohydrate; 1 g Fibre; 14 g Protein; 480 mg Sodium

Pictured at right.

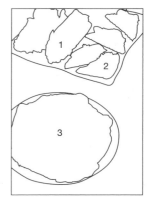

1. Turkey Romaine Spears, page 14
2. Smoked Salmon Triangles, page 21
3. Oven-Baked Brie, above

Mushroom Lentil Tapenade

A bold blend of mushrooms, olives and sun-dried tomatoes that can be served with crackers or toasted baguette slices. This convenient dip is made in advance and chilled until your company arrives.

Olive (or cooking) oil	1 tbsp.	15 mL
Chopped fresh brown	4 cups	1 L
(or white) mushrooms		
Dried thyme	1 tsp.	5 mL
Can of lentils, rinsed and drained	19 oz.	540 mL
Chopped pitted kalamata olives	1 cup	250 mL
Sun-dried tomato pesto	3 tbsp.	50 mL
Olive (or cooking) oil	2 tbsp.	30 mL
Lemon juice	2 tsp.	10 mL
Coarsely ground pepper	1/2 tsp.	2 mL
Garlic clove, minced	1	1
(or 1/4 tsp., 1 mL, powder)		

Heat first amount of olive oil in large frying pan on medium-high. Add mushrooms and thyme. Cook for about 10 minutes, stirring often, until liquid is evaporated and mushrooms are browned. Cool. Transfer to food processor.

Add remaining 7 ingredients. Process with on/off motion, scraping down sides if necessary, until almost smooth. Chill, covered, for at least 6 hours or overnight. Makes about 4 cups (1 L).

1/4 cup (60 mL): 65 Calories; 3.6 g Total Fat (2.2 g Mono, 0.9 g Poly, 0.3 g Sat); 0 mg Cholesterol; 6 g Carbohydrate; 3 g Fibre; 3 g Protein; 143 mg Sodium

1. Cranorange Tea, page 23
2. Hazelnut Eggnog Latte, page 24
3. Espresso Shortbread, page 129
4. Holiday Fruit Punch, page 22

Props: Le Gnome

Chili Pecans

Toasty pecans with a spicy bite—perfect for wrapping up for gifts or stocking stuffers. Store these in an airtight container at room temperature for up to three weeks, or in the freezer for up to two months.

Egg white (large)	1	1
Maple (or maple-flavoured) syrup	1 tbsp.	15 mL
Coarse salt	1 tsp.	5 mL
Chili powder	3/4 tsp.	4 mL
Dried crushed chilies	1/2 tsp.	2 mL
Ground cumin	1/4 tsp.	1 mL
Pecan halves	3 cups	750 mL

Combine first 6 ingredients in medium bowl.

Add pecans. Stir until coated. Spread evenly on greased baking sheet with sides. Bake in 300°F (150°C) oven for about 25 minutes, stirring occasionally, until golden and fragrant. Makes about 3 cups (750 mL).

1/4 cup (60 mL): 193 Calories; 19.5 g Total Fat (11.0 g Mono, 5.8 g Poly, 1.7 g Sat); 0 mg Cholesterol; 5 g Carbohydrate; 3 g Fibre; 3 g Protein; 199 mg Sodium

Winter White Bean Dip

Everyone will flock to this creamy bean dip on the buffet table—it's rich with garlic cream cheese, yet has a light, lemony flavour.

Can of white kidney beans, rinsed and drained	19 oz.	540 mL
Lemon juice	2 tbsp.	30 mL
Ground cumin	2 tsp.	10 mL
Tub of herb and garlic cream cheese	8 oz.	250 g

Process first 3 ingredients in food processor until smooth. Transfer to small bowl.

Add cream cheese. Mix well. Makes about 2 1/2 cups (625 mL).

1/4 cup (60 mL): 116 Calories; 7.7 g Total Fat (0 g Mono, 0 g Poly, 4.6 g Sat); 31 mg Cholesterol; 9 g Carbohydrate; 2 g Fibre; 4 g Protein; 157 mg Sodium

Appetizers & Snacks

Smoked Salmon Triangles

Smoked salmon and herb-speckled cream cheese are simply made for each other. This classic combo creates colourful appetizers that will disappear fast!

Spreadable cream cheese	1 cup	250 mL
Chopped fresh parsley	1/4 cup	60 mL
(or 1 1/2 tsp., 7 mL, flakes)		
Chopped fresh dill (or 1 1/2 tsp.,	2 tbsp.	30 mL
7 mL, dried)		
Lemon juice	1 tbsp.	15 mL
Grated lemon zest (see Tip, page 152)	1 tsp.	5 mL
Pepper	1/4 tsp.	1 mL
Pumpernickel cocktail bread slices	16	16
Smoked salmon slices (about 8 oz.,	32	32
225 g), larger ones halved		
Parsley (or dill) sprigs	32	32
Coarsely ground black pepper,		
for garnish		

Combine first 6 ingredients in small bowl.

Spread over bread slices. Cut slices in half diagonally.

Roll 1 slice of salmon into cone shape. Place, seam-side down, on 1 bread half. Place 1 parsley sprig inside cone. Repeat with remaining salmon slices, bread halves and parsley sprigs.

Sprinkle with pepper. Makes 32 triangles.

1 triangle: 43 Calories; 3.0 g Total Fat (0.9 g Mono, 0.2 g Poly, 1.7 g Sat); 10 mg Cholesterol; 2 g Carbohydrate; trace Fibre; 2 g Protein; 101 mg Sodium

Pictured on front cover and on page 17.

Paré Pointer

His manners have improved since he started to work in a refinery.

Holiday Fruit Punch

A classic punch for the buffet table. Add some festive sparkle with frozen cranberries or frozen pineapple rings—a beautiful garnish that keeps your punch cold without watering it down.

Pineapple juice, chilled	4 cups	1 L
Can of frozen concentrated orange juice	12 1/2 oz.	355 mL
Can of frozen concentrated pink lemonade	12 1/2 oz.	355 mL
Ginger ale, chilled	8 cups	2 L

Combine first 3 ingredients in large punch bowl.

Add ginger ale. Stir gently. Makes about 15 cups (3.75 L).

1 cup (250 mL): 162 Calories; 0.1 g Total Fat (0 g Mono, trace Poly, trace Sat); 0 mg Cholesterol; 42 g Carbohydrate; trace Fibre; 1 g Protein; 18 mg Sodium

Pictured on page 18.

Vanilla Chai Tea Liqueur

Spread the cheer on Christmas Eve by serving this fragrant, warming liqueur in small tumblers, or by pouring it into attractive bottles and sending it home with guests. It can be mixed with milk or cream and served over ice, or added to tea or hot milk.

Vanilla bean, split lengthwise	1	1
Vodka (50% alcohol)	1 1/2 cups	375 mL
White (light) rum	1 1/2 cups	375 mL
Minced crystallized ginger	2 tbsp.	30 mL
Whole black peppercorns	2 tsp.	10 mL
Ceylon tea bags	4	4
Cinnamon sticks (4 inches, 10 cm, each)	4	4
Whole green cardamom, bruised (see Tip, page 26)	6	6
Whole cloves	6	6
Brown sugar, packed	1 cup	250 mL
Water	1/2 cup	125 mL

(continued on next page)

Place vanilla bean in sterile 1 quart (1 L) jar with tight-fitting lid.

Add next 8 ingredients. Seal jar. Let stand at room temperature for 24 hours. Remove and discard tea bags. Seal jar. Let stand at room temperature for 2 weeks. Strain through 4 layers of cheesecloth into 4 cup (1 L) liquid measure. Discard solids. Return vodka mixture to same jar.

Bring sugar and water to a boil in small saucepan, stirring constantly until sugar is dissolved. Remove from heat. Cool. Add to vodka mixture. Seal jar. Let stand at room temperature for 2 weeks. Pour into sterile jars or decorative bottles with tight-fitting lids. Makes about 34 oz. (1 L).

1 oz. (30 mL): 77 Calories; 0 g Total Fat (0 g Mono, 0 g Poly, 0 g Sat); 0 mg Cholesterol; 6 g Carbohydrate; 0 g Fibre; 0 g Protein; trace Sodium

Cranorange Tea

This surprisingly vibrant tea blend combines the bold flavours of cranberry and orange with the warmth of cinnamon. Use slices of blood orange for a particularly striking garnish.

Water	3 cups	750 mL
Can of frozen concentrated cranberry cocktail	9 1/2 oz.	275 mL
Frozen concentrated orange juice	1/2 cup	125 mL
Granulated sugar	1/4 cup	60 mL
Cinnamon sticks (4 inches, 10 cm, each)	2	2
Orange pekoe tea bags	4	4
Orange slices, halved, for garnish		

Bring first 5 ingredients to a boil in medium saucepan. Reduce heat to medium. Boil gently, uncovered, for about 5 minutes until cinnamon is fragrant. Remove from heat.

Add tea bags. Let stand, covered, for 5 minutes. Remove and discard solids with slotted spoon.

Garnish individual servings with orange slices. Makes about 4 1/2 cups (1.1 L).

1 cup (250 mL): 191 Calories; 0 g Total Fat (0 g Mono, 0 g Poly, 0 g Sat); 0 mg Cholesterol; 50 g Carbohydrate; trace Fibre; trace Protein; 4 mg Sodium

Pictured on page 18.

Cardamom Hot Chocolate

A rich, creamy hot chocolate spiced with mild cardamom—quite simply prepared with the help of your slow cooker! Try it with a splash of hazelnut liqueur or Irish cream to round out the sweet flavours.

Water	4 1/2 cups	1.1 L
Can of evaporated milk	13 oz.	370 mL
Skim milk powder	1 cup	250 mL
Cocoa, sifted if lumpy	1/4 cup	60 mL
Granulated sugar	1/4 cup	60 mL
Vanilla extract	1 tsp.	5 mL
Whole green cardamom, bruised (see Tip, page 26)	3	3
Salt	1/8 tsp.	0.5 mL
Bittersweet chocolate baking squares (1 oz., 28 g, each), chopped	3	3
Whipped cream, for garnish		

Combine first 8 ingredients in 3 1/2 to 4 quart (3.5 to 4 L) slow cooker. Cook, covered, on Low for 4 to 5 hours or on High for 2 to 2 1/2 hours. Remove and discard cardamom with slotted spoon.

Add chocolate. Whisk until smooth.

Garnish individual servings with whipped cream. Makes about 6 3/4 cups (1.7 L).

1 cup (250 mL): 214 Calories; 5.9 g Total Fat (1.5 g Mono, 0.3 g Poly, 3.9 g Sat); 17 mg Cholesterol; 31 g Carbohydrate; 2 g Fibre; 11 g Protein; 197 mg Sodium

Hazelnut Eggnog Latte

This sweet and creamy treat is a decadent way to start Christmas morning, or to welcome guests in from the cold. Balance the sweetness to your own taste by adding more or less coffee.

Hot strong prepared coffee	5 cups	1.25 L
Chocolate hazelnut spread	1 cup	250 mL
Eggnog	4 cups	1 L

(continued on next page)

Beverages

Whisk coffee and chocolate hazelnut spread in large saucepan on medium until smooth.

Add eggnog. Heat and stir until hot, but not boiling. Makes about 10 cups (2.5 L).

1 cup (250 mL): 230 Calories; 12.7 g Total Fat (5.1 g Mono, 1.5 g Poly, 5.4 g Sat); 60 mg Cholesterol; 24 g Carbohydrate; 1 g Fibre; 5 g Protein; 64 mg Sodium

Pictured on page 18.

Holiday Cran-Apple Schnapps

Smooth, sweet schnapps with a warming effect that's sure to boost your holiday cheer! This also makes a lovely gift, and creates a fabulous cocktail when combined with white cranberry cocktail and club soda.

Chopped unpeeled cooking apple (such as McIntosh), see Note 1	2 cups	500 mL
Fresh (or frozen) cranberries	1 cup	250 mL
Grated lemon zest	1 tbsp.	15 mL
Vodka (see Note 2)	3 cups	750 mL
Granulated sugar	1/2 cup	125 mL
Water	1/3 cup	75 mL

Combine first 3 ingredients in sterile 2 quart (2 L) jar with tight-fitting lid.

Add vodka. Seal jar. Shake gently. Let stand at room temperature for 4 weeks, shaking gently once every week. Strain through double layer of cheesecloth into 4 cup (1 L) liquid measure. Discard solids. Return vodka mixture to same jar.

Bring sugar and water to a boil in small saucepan, stirring constantly until sugar is dissolved. Remove from heat. Cool. Add to vodka mixture. Seal jar. Let stand at room temperature for 4 weeks. Strain through double layer of cheesecloth into 4 cup (1 L) liquid measure. Discard solids. Pour into sterile jars or decorative bottles with tight-fitting lids. Makes about 28 oz. (800 mL).

1 oz. (30 mL): 84 Calories; 0 g Total Fat (0 g Mono, 0 g Poly, 0 g Sat); 0 mg Cholesterol; 3 g Carbohydrate; 0 g Fibre; 0 g Protein; trace Sodium

Note 1: Scrub apples with a vegetable brush in hot water to remove any pesticide or wax residues.

Note 2: The best quality (and most expensive) alcohol is not necessary, but avoid the cheaper brands as they can be harsh and bitter.

Festive Eggnog

This thick and creamy eggnog has a surprisingly light flavour, with orange zest giving it a lift. Enjoy it with orange liqueur, brandy or rum if desired.

Milk	2 cups	500 mL
Grated orange zest	1/2 tsp.	2 mL
Egg yolks (large)	5	5
Milk	2 cups	500 mL
Granulated sugar	3/4 cup	175 mL
Cornstarch	3 tbsp.	50 mL
Salt	1/8 tsp.	0.5 mL
Milk	4 cups	1 L
Vanilla extract	2 tsp.	10 mL
Ground cinnamon	1/2 tsp.	2 mL
Ground cloves	1/4 tsp.	1 mL
Whipping cream	1 cup	250 mL
Ground nutmeg, sprinkle		

Combine first amount of milk and orange zest in medium saucepan. Cook on medium for about 8 minutes, stirring occasionally, until hot, but not boiling.

Beat next 5 ingredients in medium bowl. Slowly add hot milk mixture, stirring constantly. Return to saucepan. Cook on medium for about 10 minutes, stirring constantly, until boiling and thickened. Heat and stir for 2 minutes. Transfer to large bowl.

Add next 4 ingredients. Stir until combined. Let stand for 10 minutes. Chill.

Beat whipping cream in small bowl until soft peaks form. Spoon into large punch bowl. Slowly whisk in milk mixture. Sprinkle with nutmeg. Makes about 8 cups (2 L).

1 cup (250 mL): 306 Calories; 16.3 g Total Fat (5.4 g Mono, 0.9 g Poly, 9.4 g Sat); 184 mg Cholesterol; 31 g Carbohydrate; trace Fibre; 11 g Protein; 184 mg Sodium

 tip To bruise cardamom, pound pods with mallet or press with flat side of wide knife to "bruise," or crack them open slightly.

Ginger Quick Bread

Enjoy rich, gingery flavour and moist texture, all with an appealing almond and brown sugar crumble on top. This is easy to whip up if company is on the way, and is also suitable for gifting.

Ingredient	Imperial	Metric
All-purpose flour	2 cups	500 mL
Ground cinnamon	2 tsp.	10 mL
Ground ginger	2 tsp.	10 mL
Baking powder	1 1/2 tsp.	7 mL
Baking soda	1/2 tsp.	2 mL
Salt	1/2 tsp.	2 mL
Ground allspice	1/4 tsp.	1 mL
Ground cloves	1/8 tsp.	0.5 mL
Large eggs, fork-beaten	2	2
Brown sugar, packed	1/2 cup	125 mL
Buttermilk (or soured milk, see Tip, page 30)	1/2 cup	125 mL
Fancy (mild) molasses	1/2 cup	125 mL
Unsweetened applesauce	1/2 cup	125 mL
Cooking oil	1/4 cup	60 mL
Minced crystallized ginger	3 tbsp.	50 mL
Whole natural almonds, chopped	1/3 cup	75 mL
Brown sugar, packed	2 tbsp.	30 mL

Combine first 8 ingredients in large bowl. Make a well in centre.

Stir next 7 ingredients in medium bowl. Add to well. Stir until just moistened. Spread evenly in greased 9 x 5 x 3 inch (23 x 12.5 x 7.5 cm) loaf pan.

Combine almonds and second amount of brown sugar in small bowl. Sprinkle over top. Bake in 350°F (175°C) oven for about 50 minutes until wooden pick inserted in centre comes out clean. Let stand in pan for 10 minutes before removing to wire rack to cool. Cuts into 16 slices.

1 slice: 178 Calories; 5.3 g Total Fat (3.0 g Mono, 1.4 g Poly, 0.6 g Sat); 27 mg Cholesterol; 31 g Carbohydrate; 1 g Fibre; 3 g Protein; 184 mg Sodium

Pictured on page 35.

Light Rye Rolls

These golden-speckled buns will look lovely served alongside your main course.

Warm water (see Tip, page 43)	1/4 cup	60 mL
Granulated sugar	1 tsp.	5 mL
Envelope of active dry yeast	1/4 oz.	8 g
(or 2 1/4 tsp., 11 mL)		
All-purpose flour	4 cups	1 L
Light rye flour	2 cups	500 mL
Wheat germ, toasted (see Note)	3/4 cup	175 mL
Brown sugar, packed	1/4 cup	60 mL
Salt	1 1/2 tsp.	7 mL
Large egg, fork-beaten	1	1
Egg yolk, large	1	1
Warm water	1 1/2 cups	375 mL
Butter (or hard margarine), melted	1/2 cup	125 mL
All-purpose flour, approximately	3 tbsp.	50 mL
Egg white, large	1	1
Water	1 tsp.	5 mL
Wheat germ (optional)	2 tbsp.	30 mL

Stir first amount of warm water and granulated sugar in small bowl until sugar is dissolved. Sprinkle yeast over top. Let stand for 10 minutes. Stir until yeast is dissolved.

Combine next 5 ingredients in extra-large bowl. Make a well in centre.

Add next 4 ingredients and yeast mixture to well. Mix until soft dough forms. Turn out dough onto lightly floured surface.

Knead for 5 to 10 minutes until smooth and elastic, adding second amount of all-purpose flour, 1 tbsp. (15 mL) at a time, if necessary, to prevent sticking. Place in greased extra-large bowl, turning once to grease top. Cover with greased waxed paper and tea towel. Let stand in oven with light on and door closed for about 45 minutes until doubled in bulk. Punch dough down. Turn out onto lightly floured surface. Knead for about 1 minute until smooth. Divide into 24 portions. Roll into balls. Arrange, evenly spaced apart, on large greased baking sheet. Cover with greased waxed paper and tea towel. Let stand in oven with light on and door closed for about 30 minutes until almost doubled in size.

(continued on next page)

Breads

Stir egg white and water in small bowl. Brush over top. Sprinkle with wheat germ. Bake in 375°F (190°C) oven for about 20 minutes until golden and hollow sounding when tapped. Remove rolls from baking sheet. Transfer to wire rack to cool. Makes 24 rolls.

1 roll: 167 Calories; 4.9 g Total Fat (1.2 g Mono, 0.3 g Poly, 2.6 g Sat); 27 mg Cholesterol; 27 g Carbohydrate; 4 g Fibre; 5 g Protein; 179 mg Sodium

Pictured on page 107.

Note: To toast wheat germ, spread evenly in an ungreased shallow frying pan. Heat and stir on medium until golden. Cool before adding to recipe.

Hermit Muffins

These spiced muffins have a similar flavour and texture to hermit cookies.

Dark raisins	1 cup	250 mL
Boiling water	1 cup	250 mL
All-purpose flour	2 cups	500 mL
Brown sugar, packed	2/3 cup	150 mL
Baking powder	1 tbsp.	15 mL
Baking soda	1/2 tsp.	2 mL
Ground cinnamon	1/2 tsp.	2 mL
Salt	1/2 tsp.	2 mL
Ground allspice	1/4 tsp.	1 mL
Ground nutmeg	1/4 tsp.	1 mL
Large egg, fork-beaten	1	1
Butter (or hard margarine), melted	1/2 cup	125 mL
Milk	1/2 cup	125 mL
Vanilla extract	1 tsp.	5 mL

Combine raisins and boiling water in small heatproof bowl. Let stand, uncovered, for 15 minutes. Drain.

Measure next 8 ingredients into large bowl. Stir. Make a well in centre.

Combine remaining 4 ingredients in medium bowl. Add to well. Add raisins. Stir until just moistened. Fill 12 greased muffin cups 3/4 full. Bake in 375°F (190°C) oven for about 18 minutes until wooden pick inserted in centre of muffin comes out clean. Let stand in pan for 5 minutes before removing to wire rack to cool. Makes 12 muffins.

1 muffin: 252 Calories; 8.9 g Total Fat (2.6 g Mono, 0.5 g Poly, 5.3 g Sat); 40 mg Cholesterol; 41 g Carbohydrate; 1 g Fibre; 4 g Protein; 345 mg Sodium

Breads

Chocolate Toffee Muffins

These cake-like muffins have bits of toffee and a sweet caramel glaze. Treat yourself to one after a busy day of last-minute shopping.

All-purpose flour	2 cups	500 mL
Cocoa, sifted if lumpy	1/3 cup	75 mL
Baking soda	1 tsp.	5 mL
Salt	1/4 tsp.	1 mL
Buttermilk (or soured milk, see Tip, below)	2/3 cup	150 mL
Vanilla extract	1 tsp.	5 mL
Butter (or hard margarine), softened	1/2 cup	125 mL
Granulated sugar	1 cup	250 mL
Large eggs	2	2
Toffee bits (such as Skor)	1/2 cup	125 mL
Caramel ice cream topping	1/4 cup	60 mL

Combine first 4 ingredients in medium bowl.

Combine buttermilk and vanilla in small bowl.

Beat butter and sugar in large bowl until light and fluffy. Add eggs 1 at a time, beating well after each addition.

Add flour mixture in 3 parts, alternating with buttermilk mixture in 2 parts, adding toffee bits with last addition. Stir well after each addition until just combined. Fill 12 greased muffin cups 3/4 full. Bake in 375°F (190°C) oven for about 20 minutes until wooden pick inserted in centre of muffin comes out clean.

Drizzle caramel topping over muffins. Let stand in pan for 5 minutes before removing to wire rack to cool. Makes 12 muffins.

1 muffin: 295 Calories; 11.8 g Total Fat (2.8 g Mono, 0.5 g Poly, 5.6 g Sat); 62 mg Cholesterol; 45 g Carbohydrate; 1 g Fibre; 5 g Protein; 304 mg Sodium

 tip To make soured milk, measure 1 tbsp. (15 mL) white vinegar or lemon juice into a 1 cup (250 mL) liquid measure. Add enough milk to make 1 cup (250 mL). Stir. Let stand for 1 minute.

Fruit and Nut Loaf

This nutritious loaf makes for a smart choice on Christmas morning.

Chopped dried apple	1/2 cup	125 mL
Chopped dried apricot	1/2 cup	125 mL
Chopped dried pineapple	1/4 cup	60 mL
Boiling water	1 1/2 cups	375 mL
All-purpose flour	1 1/2 cups	375 mL
Chopped pecans, toasted (see Tip, page 99)	1/2 cup	125 mL
Granulated sugar	1/2 cup	125 mL
Whole-wheat flour	1/2 cup	125 mL
Baking powder	1 1/2 tsp.	7 mL
Salt	1/2 tsp.	2 mL
Baking soda	1/4 tsp.	1 mL
Large egg	1	1
Pineapple juice	1/2 cup	125 mL
Unsweetened applesauce	1/2 cup	125 mL
Cooking oil	3 tbsp.	50 mL
Vanilla extract	1 tsp.	5 mL

Combine first 4 ingredients in medium heatproof bowl. Let stand, uncovered, for about 10 minutes until softened. Drain.

Combine next 7 ingredients in large bowl. Make a well in centre.

Beat remaining 5 ingredients in medium bowl. Add apricot mixture. Stir. Add to well. Stir until just moistened. Spread evenly in greased 9 x 5 x 3 inch (23 x 12.5 x 7.5 cm) loaf pan. Bake in 350°F (175°C) oven for about 55 minutes until wooden pick inserted in centre comes out clean. Let stand in pan for 10 minutes before removing to wire rack to cool. Cuts into 16 slices.

1 slice: 158 Calories; 5.7 g Total Fat (3.2 g Mono, 1.7 g Poly, 0.5 g Sat); 13 mg Cholesterol; 26 g Carbohydrate; 2 g Fibre; 3 g Protein; 186 mg Sodium

Panettone Braid

A beautiful braided ring with raisins and candied peel, ideal for special holiday gatherings. Saffron may be a little pricey, but the subtle floral notes and lovely yellow hue it lends to this traditional Italian bread are worth it!

Milk	1/2 cup	125 mL
Granulated sugar	1 1/2 tsp.	7 mL
Saffron threads, pinch (optional)		
Envelope of active dry yeast (or 2 1/4 tsp., 11 mL)	1/4 oz.	8 g
Large eggs, fork-beaten	2	2
All-purpose flour	2 1/2 cups	625 mL
Butter (or hard margarine), melted	1/4 cup	60 mL
Granulated sugar	1/4 cup	60 mL
Grated lemon zest	1 tsp.	5 mL
Salt	1/2 tsp.	2 mL
Chopped mixed glazed fruit	1/3 cup	75 mL
Sultana raisins	1/4 cup	60 mL
Chopped pine nuts, toasted (see Tip, page 99)	3 tbsp.	50 mL
All-purpose flour	1/4 cup	60 mL
Butter (or hard margarine), melted	1 tbsp.	15 mL

Combine first 3 ingredients in small saucepan. Heat and stir on medium for about 4 minutes until sugar is dissolved and milk is hot, but not boiling. Transfer to extra-large bowl. Let stand for 5 minutes (see Tip, page 43).

Sprinkle with yeast. Let stand for 10 minutes. Stir until yeast is dissolved.

Add next 6 ingredients. Stir until soft dough forms.

(continued on next page)

Add next 3 ingredients. Knead, adding second amount of flour, 1 tbsp. (15 mL) at a time, until stiff dough forms. Turn out onto work surface. Knead for 5 to 10 minutes until smooth and elastic. Place in greased large bowl, turning once to grease top. Cover with greased waxed paper and tea towel. Let stand in oven with light on and door closed for about 1 1/2 hours until doubled in bulk. Punch dough down. Turn out onto lightly floured surface. Divide dough into 3 equal portions. Roll into 24 inch (60 cm) long ropes. Place ropes, side-by-side, on work surface. Pinch ropes together at one end. Braid. Pinch together at opposite end. Place in greased 10 inch (25 cm) angel food tube pan. Pinch ends together to form ring. Cover with greased waxed paper and tea towel. Let stand in oven with light on and door closed for about 1 hour until doubled in size. Bake in 350°F (175°C) oven for about 35 minutes until golden brown and hollow sounding when tapped. Remove from pan. Transfer to wire rack.

Brush with second amount of butter. Cool. Cuts into 16 pieces.

1 piece: 156 Calories; 5.4 g Total Fat (1.5 g Mono, 0.8 g Poly, 2.6 g Sat); 36 mg Cholesterol; 24 g Carbohydrate; 1 g Fibre; 4 g Protein; 117 mg Sodium

Paré Pointer

The limestone wished that the construction workers would stop taking it for granite.

Breads

Savoury Herb Biscuits

Everyone enjoys a good, simple biscuit with their meal. These golden biscuits are fluffy with a nice herb flavour—very versatile.

All-purpose flour	2 cups	500 mL
Baking powder	2 tsp.	10 mL
Dried oregano	1 tsp.	10 mL
Dried thyme	1 tsp.	10 mL
Granulated sugar	1 tsp.	10 mL
Baking soda	1/2 tsp.	2 mL
Salt	1/4 tsp.	1 mL
Pepper	1/8 tsp.	0.5 mL
Cold butter (or hard margarine), cut up	1/2 cup	125 mL
Large egg, fork-beaten	1	1
Buttermilk (or soured milk, see Tip, page 30)	3/4 cup	175 mL

Combine first 8 ingredients in large bowl. Cut in butter until mixture resembles coarse crumbs. Make a well in centre.

Add egg and buttermilk to well. Stir until soft dough forms. Turn out onto lightly floured surface. Knead 8 times. Roll or pat out to 1/2 inch (12 mm) thickness. Cut out circles with lightly floured 2 inch (5 cm) biscuit cutter. Arrange about 1 inch (2.5 cm) apart on greased baking sheet. Bake in 400°F (205°C) oven for about 12 minutes until golden. Makes about 24 biscuits.

1 biscuit: 76 Calories; 4.2 g Total Fat (1.1 g Mono, 0.2 g Poly, 2.6 g Sat); 19 mg Cholesterol; 8 g Carbohydrate; trace Fibre; 2 g Protein; 133 mg Sodium

1. Christmas Pudding Pull-Aparts, page 39
2. Ginger Quick Bread, page 27
3. Stollen, page 40

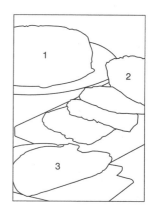

Breads

Pesto Pizza Pinwheels

Gourmet pizza flavour rolled into a spiral! These can be made ahead and reheated. For best results, be sure to blot all moisture from the peppers.

Tube of refrigerator pizza dough	13.8 oz.	391 g
Basil pesto	1/4 cup	60 mL
Chopped roasted red peppers, blotted dry	1/2 cup	125 mL
Grated Asiago (or mozzarella) cheese	1/3 cup	75 mL

Unroll dough into rectangle. Spread pesto over top, leaving 1/2 inch (12 mm) edge on 1 short side.

Scatter red pepper over pesto. Roll up, jelly-roll style, from covered short side. Press seam against roll to seal. Cut into 1 inch (2.5 cm) slices. Arrange, cut-side down, about 2 inches (5 cm) apart, on greased baking sheet.

Sprinkle with cheese. Bake in 350°F (175°C) oven for about 22 minutes until golden (see Note). Makes about 8 pinwheels.

1 pinwheel: 194 Calories; 6.7 g Total Fat (0 g Mono, 0 g Poly, 1.7 g Sat); 6 mg Cholesterol; 26 g Carbohydrate; 1 g Fibre; 6 g Protein; 599 mg Sodium

Note: Baked pinwheels may be made ahead and stored in an airtight container in the refrigerator for up to 24 hours. To reheat, wrap with foil and heat in a 350°F (175°C) oven for about 10 minutes until heated through.

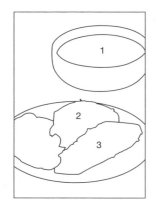

1. Roasted Butternut Soup, page 57
2. Fennel Potato Gratin, page 110
3. Honey Cajun Salmon, page 73

Props: Le Gnome

Overnight Dinner Rolls

These wholesome whole-wheat buns are prepared the day before and baked up when you need them—perfect for the hectic season.

Whole-wheat flour	2 cups	500 mL
All-purpose flour	1 2/3 cups	400 mL
Envelope of instant yeast (or 2 1/4 tsp., 11 mL)	1/4 oz.	8 g
Water	1 cup	250 mL
Milk	1/2 cup	125 mL
Cooking oil	1/4 cup	60 mL
Brown sugar, packed	2 tbsp.	30 mL
Salt	1 tsp.	5 mL
All-purpose flour, approximately	3 tbsp.	50 mL
Butter (or hard margarine), melted	2 tbsp.	30 mL

Combine first 3 ingredients in large bowl.

Combine next 5 ingredients in small saucepan on medium. Heat and stir for about 3 minutes until very warm (see Tip, page 43). Add to flour mixture. Stir until soft dough forms.

Turn out onto lightly floured surface. Knead for about 10 minutes until smooth and elastic, adding second amount of all-purpose flour, 1 tbsp. (15 mL) at a time, if necessary, to prevent sticking. Transfer to greased large bowl, turning once to grease top. Cover with greased waxed paper and tea towel. Let stand in oven with light on and door closed for 30 minutes. Turn out onto work surface. Knead for 1 minute. Divide into 18 portions. Roll into balls. Arrange balls in 2 greased 9 x 9 inch (23 x 23 cm) pans. Cover pans tightly with greased foil. Refrigerate overnight or up to 16 hours. Loosen foil. Let stand at room temperature for 30 minutes.

Brush with butter. Bake in 350°F (175°C) oven for about 30 minutes until golden brown and hollow sounding when tapped. Remove buns from pans. Place on wire racks to cool. Makes 18 buns.

1 bun: 134 Calories; 4.7 g Total Fat (2.2 g Mono, 1.1 g Poly, 1.1 g Sat); 4 mg Cholesterol; 21 g Carbohydrate; 2 g Fibre; 4 g Protein; 143 mg Sodium

Breads

Christmas Pudding Pull-Aparts

Enjoy the classic flavours of Christmas pudding in these ooey-gooey sticky buns. No one will be able to resist!

Chopped dried fruit	1/2 cup	125 mL
Sultana raisins	1/4 cup	60 mL
Brandy (or apple juice)	2 tbsp.	30 mL
Currants	2 tbsp.	30 mL
Diced mixed peel	2 tbsp.	30 mL
Brown sugar, packed	1/3 cup	75 mL
Ground cinnamon	1/4 tsp.	1 mL
Frozen white bread dough, covered, thawed in refrigerator overnight	1	1
CARAMEL SAUCE		
Brown sugar, packed	1/2 cup	125 mL
Butter (or hard margarine)	1/4 cup	60 mL
Whipping cream	1/4 cup	60 mL

Combine first 5 ingredients in small bowl. Let stand, covered, for about 1 hour, stirring once, until fruit is softened and brandy is absorbed.

Combine brown sugar and cinnamon in small cup.

Roll out dough on lightly floured surface to 8 x 15 inch (20 x 38 cm) rectangle. Sprinkle with brown sugar mixture, leaving 1/2 inch (12 mm) edge. Scatter fruit mixture over top. Roll up, jelly-roll style, from long side. Pinch seam against roll to seal. Cut into 12 slices, using serrated knife. Arrange 9 slices, cut-side down, around edge of greased 9 inch (23 cm) springform pan. Arrange remaining 3 slices in centre. Cover with greased waxed paper and tea towel. Let stand in oven with light on and door closed for about 1 1/2 hours until doubled in size. Bake in 375°F (190°C) oven for about 30 minutes until golden.

Caramel Sauce: Combine all 3 ingredients in small saucepan on medium. Heat and stir until sugar is dissolved. Bring to a boil. Reduce heat to medium-low. Simmer for about 3 minutes, without stirring, until mixture is slightly thickened. Makes about 2/3 cup (150 mL). Drizzle over pull-aparts. Makes 12 pull-aparts.

1 pull-apart: 243 Calories; 7.2 g Total Fat (1.5 g Mono, 0.2 g Poly, 3.5 g Sat); 17 mg Cholesterol; 39 g Carbohydrate; 2 g Fibre; 4 g Protein; 243 mg Sodium

Pictured on page 35.

Breads

Stollen

A gorgeous loaf with an icing sugar glaze and festive fruit peeking out. Long, elegant slices reveal soft-textured bread and a deliciously sweet almond paste centre, which lends an authentically European flavour.

Warm water (see Tip, page 43)	1/3 cup	75 mL
Granulated sugar	1 tsp.	5 mL
Envelope of active dry yeast	1/4 oz.	8 g
(or 2 1/4 tsp., 11 mL)		
All-purpose flour	2 1/2 cups	625 mL
Ground cardamom	1/2 tsp.	2 mL
Ground nutmeg	1/2 tsp.	2 mL
Salt	1/2 tsp.	2 mL
Large eggs	2	2
2% cottage cheese	2/3 cup	150 mL
Butter (or hard margarine), melted	1/3 cup	75 mL
Granulated sugar	1/3 cup	75 mL
Grated orange zest	1 tsp.	5 mL
Vanilla extract	1 tsp.	5 mL
Chopped dried cherries	1/3 cup	75 mL
Dark raisins	1/3 cup	75 mL
Dried cranberries	1/3 cup	75 mL
All-purpose flour, approximately	1/4 cup	60 mL
Almond paste	4 oz.	113 g
Butter (or hard margarine), melted	1 tbsp.	15 mL
Icing (confectioner's) sugar	2 tbsp.	30 mL

Stir water and first amount of granulated sugar in small bowl until sugar is dissolved. Sprinkle yeast over top. Let stand for 10 minutes. Stir until yeast is dissolved.

Combine next 4 ingredients in large bowl. Make a well in centre.

Process next 6 ingredients in blender or food processor until smooth. Add to well. Add yeast mixture. Mix until soft dough forms.

Add next 3 ingredients. Mix. Turn out dough onto lightly floured surface.

(continued on next page)

Breads

Knead for 5 to 10 minutes until smooth and elastic, adding second amount of flour, 1 tbsp. (15 mL) at a time, if necessary, to prevent sticking. Place in greased extra-large bowl, turning once to grease top. Cover with greased waxed paper and tea towel. Let stand in oven with light on and door closed for about 1 hour until doubled in bulk. Punch dough down. Turn out onto lightly floured surface. Knead for about 1 minute until smooth. Roll out to 8 x 12 inch (20 x 30 cm) oval.

Roll out almond paste to 5 inch (12.5 cm) circle. Place on one narrow end of oval, leaving 1 inch (2.5 cm) edge (see Diagram). Fold dough over to enclose filling. Pinch edges to seal. Place on greased baking sheet. Cover with greased waxed paper and tea towel. Let stand in oven with light on and door closed for about 1 hour until doubled in size. Bake in 350°F (175°C) oven for about 35 minutes until browned and hollow sounding when tapped. Let stand on baking sheet for 5 minutes before removing to wire rack to cool.

Brush with second amount of butter. Sprinkle with icing sugar. Cuts into 20 slices.

1 slice: 163 Calories; 5.9 g Total Fat (2.2 g Mono, 0.5 g Poly, 2.7 g Sat); 31 mg Cholesterol; 24 g Carbohydrate; 1 g Fibre; 4 g Protein; 124 mg Sodium

Pictured on page 35.

Make Ahead: Wrap tightly in plastic wrap and store at room temperature for 3 to 4 days. This version of stollen should not be frozen, as the almond paste filling does not maintain its texture after thawing.

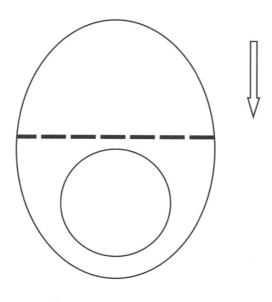

Poppy Seed Egg Bread

This whole-wheat egg bread was inspired by challah *(pronounced HAH-lah).*
Challah is traditionally served on the Jewish Sabbath day and on holidays.

All-purpose flour	3 cups	750 mL
Whole-wheat flour	1 1/4 cups	300 mL
Poppy seeds	1/4 cup	60 mL
Envelope of instant yeast	1/4 oz.	8 g
(or 2 1/4 tsp., 11 mL)		
Large eggs	2	2
Egg yolks, large	2	2
Very warm water (see Tip, right)	1 cup	250 mL
Liquid honey	3 tbsp.	50 mL
Cooking oil	2 tbsp.	30 mL
Salt	1 tsp.	5 mL
All-purpose flour, approximately	6 tbsp.	100 mL
Egg white, large	1	1
Poppy seeds	1 tbsp.	15 mL

Combine first 4 ingredients in extra-large bowl. Make a well in centre.

Whisk next 6 ingredients in medium bowl until combined. Add to well. Mix
until soft dough forms. Turn out onto lightly floured surface.

Knead for 5 to 10 minutes until smooth and elastic, adding second amount
of all-purpose flour, 1 tbsp. (15 mL) at a time, if necessary, to prevent
sticking. Place in greased extra-large bowl, turning once to grease top.
Cover with greased waxed paper and tea towel. Let stand in oven with
light on and door closed for about 1 hour until doubled in bulk. Punch
dough down. Turn out onto work surface. Knead for about 1 minute until
smooth. Divide dough into 3 equal portions. Roll portions into 16 inch
(40 cm) long ropes. Place ropes, side-by-side, on greased baking sheet.
Pinch ropes together at one end. Braid. Pinch together at opposite end.
Cover with greased waxed paper and tea towel. Let stand in oven with
light on and door closed for about 45 minutes until doubled in size.

Beat egg white in small bowl. Brush over top. Sprinkle with poppy seeds.
Bake in 375°F (190°C) oven for about 30 minutes until golden brown and
hollow sounding when tapped. Remove bread from pan. Transfer to wire
rack to cool. Cuts into 20 slices.

1 slice: 141 Calories; 3.4 g Total Fat (1.4 g Mono, 1.3 g Poly, 0.5 g Sat); 42 mg Cholesterol;
24 g Carbohydrate; 2 g Fibre; 5 g Protein; 123 mg Sodium

Chèvre Pear Quesadillas

Start Christmas day the gourmet way! These quesadillas whip up quick with crisp tortillas, goat cheese and pears—a delicious blend of sweet and savoury ingredients that creates an elegant brunch option.

Soft goat (chèvre) cheese	1/2 cup	125 mL
Chopped fresh basil	3 tbsp.	50 mL
Liquid honey	2 tsp.	10 mL
Whole-wheat flour tortillas (10 inch, 25 cm, diameter)	4	4
Medium unpeeled pears, sliced	2	2
Balsamic vinegar	1 tbsp.	15 mL

Combine first 3 ingredients in small bowl. Spread over tortillas, almost to edge.

Arrange pear over half of each tortilla.

Brush vinegar over pear. Fold tortillas in half to cover filling. Press down lightly. Arrange on greased baking sheets with sides. Cook in 425°F (220°C) oven for about 12 minutes until filling is heated through and edges are crisp. Cut into 4 wedges each, for a total of 16 wedges.

1 wedge: 74 Calories; 2.4 g Total Fat (0.5 g Mono, 0.1 g Poly, 1.5 g Sat); 6 mg Cholesterol; 13 g Carbohydrate; 1 g Fibre; 3 g Protein; 113 mg Sodium

 tip   When using yeast, it is important for the liquid to be at the correct temperature. If the liquid is too cool, the yeast will not activate properly. If the liquid is too hot, the yeast will be destroyed. For best results, follow the recommended temperatures as instructed on the package.

Crispy Hash Brown Chicken

This one's for the hash brown lovers—an intriguing combination of tender chicken combined with the crispy, golden-brown brunch favourite.

Boneless, skinless chicken breast halves (4 – 6 oz., 113 – 170 g, each)	4	4
Salt, sprinkle		
Pepper, sprinkle		
Frozen shredded hash brown potatoes, thawed	1 1/2 cups	375 mL
Grated Parmesan cheese	3 tbsp.	50 mL
Mayonnaise	3 tbsp.	50 mL
Chopped fresh parsley (or 3/4 tsp., 4 mL, flakes)	1 tbsp.	15 mL
Finely chopped green onion	1 tbsp.	15 mL
Dried dillweed	1/4 tsp.	1 mL
Salt	1/4 tsp.	1 mL
Pepper	1/4 tsp.	1 mL
Paprika, sprinkle		

Sprinkle both sides of chicken breasts with salt and pepper. Arrange on greased baking sheet with sides.

Combine next 8 ingredients in medium bowl. Spread over chicken.

Sprinkle with paprika. Cook in 400°F (205°C) oven for about 35 minutes until potato is golden and internal temperature of chicken reaches 170°F (77°C). Serves 4.

1 serving: 343 Calories; 23.6 g Total Fat (2.5 g Mono, 1.0 g Poly, 5.5 g Sat); 76 mg Cholesterol; 11 g Carbohydrate; 1 g Fibre; 28 g Protein; 486 mg Sodium

Paré Pointer

If you find a button in your salad, it probably fell off while the salad was dressing.

Crab and Red Pepper Quiche

A rich and decadent quiche with savoury crab, goat cheese and a touch of citrus—simply a delight for brunch guests.

Pastry for 9 inch (23 cm) deep dish pie shell		
Can of crabmeat, drained, cartilage removed, flaked	6 oz.	170 g
Goat (chèvre) cheese, cut up	3 oz.	85 g
Chopped roasted red peppers	1/4 cup	60 mL
Chopped fresh parsley (or 1 1/2 tsp., 7 mL, flakes)	2 tbsp.	30 mL
Thinly sliced green onion	2 tbsp.	30 mL
Large eggs	3	3
Milk	3/4 cup	175 mL
All-purpose flour	2 tbsp.	30 mL
Grated lemon zest	1/4 tsp.	1 mL
Cayenne pepper	1/8 tsp.	0.5 mL
Salt	1/4 tsp.	1 mL
Pepper	1/8 tsp.	0.5 mL

Roll out pastry on lightly floured surface to 1/8 inch (3 mm) thickness. Line 9 inch (23 cm) deep dish pie plate with pastry. Trim, leaving 1/2 inch (12 mm) overhang. Roll under and crimp decorative edge. Cover pastry with parchment paper, bringing paper up over edge. Fill halfway up side with dried beans. Bake on bottom rack in 375°F (190°C) oven for 15 minutes. Remove from oven. Carefully remove parchment paper and beans, reserving beans for next time you bake pastry. Bake pie shell on bottom rack for about 15 minutes until golden. Let stand on wire rack for 10 minutes.

Combine next 5 ingredients in medium bowl. Spoon into pie shell.

Beat remaining 7 ingredients in small bowl. Pour over crab mixture. Bake on middle rack in 350°F (175°C) oven for about 45 minutes until knife inserted in centre comes out clean. Let stand for 5 minutes. Cuts into 6 wedges.

1 wedge: 311 Calories; 16.7 g Total Fat (2.1 g Mono, 0.6 g Poly, 8.0 g Sat); 151 mg Cholesterol; 23 g Carbohydrate; trace Fibre; 15 g Protein; 544 mg Sodium

Pictured on page 72.

Sweet Waffle Bake

Serve brunch to a crowd with these tasty apple cinnamon waffles—they're prepared in a baking dish and popped in the oven the next morning. The kids will love to help get this ready the night before company comes!

Frozen waffles, halved	8	8
Can of apple pie filling	19 oz.	540 mL
Large eggs, fork-beaten	4	4
Milk	2 cups	500 mL
Maple (or maple-flavoured) syrup	1/2 cup	125 mL
Ground cinnamon	1/4 tsp.	1 mL

Spoon pie filling onto each waffle half. Arrange waffles, pie filling-side up, slightly overlapping, in greased 9 x 13 inch (23 x 33 cm) baking dish.

Combine next 4 ingredients in medium bowl. Pour over waffles. Chill, covered, overnight. Bake, uncovered, in 350°F (175°C) oven for about 50 minutes until set and lightly browned. Serves 8.

1 serving: 280 Calories; 6.2 g Total Fat (1.2 g Mono, 0.4 g Poly, 1.9 g Sat); 120 mg Cholesterol; 49 g Carbohydrate; 1 g Fibre; 8 g Protein; 319 mg Sodium

Granola Parfaits

Pretty parfaits to serve up for Christmas morning—a light, sweet and filling breakfast or brunch offering. Toasted coconut adds some tropical flair.

Granola	1 cup	250 mL
Mango (or peach) yogurt	1 cup	250 mL
Chopped frozen mango pieces, thawed	1 cup	250 mL
Sliced kiwi fruit	1 cup	250 mL
Fresh strawberries, quartered	1 cup	250 mL
Shredded coconut, toasted (see Tip, page 46)	4 tsp.	20 mL

Layer all 6 ingredients, in order given, in 4 parfait glasses. Makes 4 parfaits.

1 parfait: 230 Calories; 5.9 g Total Fat (0.1 g Mono, 0.2 g Poly, 1.2 g Sat); 3 mg Cholesterol; 43 g Carbohydrate; 8 g Fibre; 8 g Protein; 37 mg Sodium

Pictured on page 72.

Berry French Toast Sandwiches

Make-ahead recipes are ideal for the holidays—here's a brunch option that you put together the night before and bake the next morning. Serve these sandwiches with your favourite syrup.

Large eggs	8	8
Milk	1 1/2 cups	375 mL
Maple (or maple-flavoured) syrup	2 tbsp.	30 mL
Vanilla extract	1 tbsp.	15 mL
Ground cinnamon	1 tsp.	5 mL
Salt	1/8 tsp.	0.5 mL
French bread slices (3/4 inch, 2 cm, thick)	6	6
Fresh (or frozen) blueberries	1 cup	250 mL
Block cream cheese, diced	4 oz.	125 g
French bread slices (3/4 inch, 2 cm, thick)	6	6
Maple (or maple-flavoured) syrup, warmed	1/2 cup	125 mL

Beat first 6 ingredients in large bowl until smooth.

Dip first amount of bread slices into egg mixture. Arrange in single layer in well-greased 9 x 13 inch (23 x 33 cm) pan. Scatter blueberries and cream cheese over top.

Dip second amount of bread slices into egg mixture. Arrange over cream cheese mixture. Pour any remaining egg mixture over sandwiches. Chill, covered, overnight. Bake, covered, in 350°F (175°C) oven for 30 minutes. Remove cover. Bake for about 30 minutes until golden. Let stand for 5 minutes.

Drizzle with second amount of syrup. Makes 6 sandwiches.

1 sandwich: 650 Calories; 17.8 g Total Fat (6.2 g Mono, 2.1 g Poly, 7.4 g Sat); 307 mg Cholesterol; 97 g Carbohydrate; 5 g Fibre; 24 g Protein; 1013 mg Sodium

Variation: Use your favourite frozen berries instead of blueberries.

Cranberry Orange Blintzes

These crepe packets, Jewish in origin, are filled with a light, cream-cheesy filling. They're prepared ahead and chilled overnight—just pop them in the oven and heat the tangy-sweet orange cranberry sauce while you wait!

Ricotta cheese	2 cups	500 mL
Large eggs	3	3
All-purpose flour	1 1/3 cups	325 mL
Milk	1 1/3 cups	325 mL
Butter (or hard margarine), melted	2 tbsp.	30 mL
Orange liqueur	1 tbsp.	15 mL
Salt, just a pinch		
Cooking oil	1 tbsp.	15 mL
Block cream cheese, softened	4 oz.	125 g
Icing (confectioner's) sugar	2 tbsp.	30 mL
Cornstarch	1 tbsp.	15 mL
Grated orange zest (see Tip, page 152)	1/2 tsp.	2 mL
Whole cranberry sauce	1 cup	250 mL
Orange juice	3 tbsp.	50 mL
Orange liqueur	2 tsp.	10 mL
Grated orange zest	1/8 tsp.	0.5 mL

Line medium sieve with coffee filter (or paper towel). Place over medium deep bowl. Spoon ricotta into filter. Chill, covered, for 2 hours. Discard liquid.

Process next 6 ingredients in blender or food processor until smooth. Transfer to small bowl. Chill, covered, for 1 hour.

Heat 1/4 tsp. (1 mL) cooking oil in small non-stick frying pan on medium. Stir batter. Pour about 3 tbsp. (50 mL) batter into pan. Immediately tilt and swirl pan to ensure bottom is covered. Cook for 1 to 2 minutes until top is set and brown spots appear on bottom. Turn crepe over. Cook for 30 seconds. Transfer to plate. Repeat with remaining cooking oil and batter. Makes about 12 crepes.

(continued on next page)

Stir next 4 ingredients and ricotta in medium bowl until smooth. Arrange crepes on work surface. Spoon about 3 tbsp. (50 mL) ricotta mixture in centre of each crepe. Fold in sides. Fold up from bottoms to make rectangular parcels. Arrange parcels, seam-side down, in greased 9 x 13 inch (23 x 33 cm) baking dish. Chill, covered, overnight. Bake, uncovered, in 375°F (190°C) oven for about 20 minutes until heated through.

Combine remaining 4 ingredients in medium saucepan on medium-low. Cook for about 8 minutes, stirring occasionally, until heated through. Serve with blintzes. Serves 6.

1 serving: 502 Calories; 25.1 g Total Fat (5.4 g Mono, 1.4 g Poly, 13.8 g Sat); 173 mg Cholesterol; 47 g Carbohydrate; 1 g Fibre; 20 g Protein; 291 mg Sodium

Pictured on page 72.

Festive Fruit Medley

Who doesn't love fresh fruit with breakfast? This sweet medley is topped with a dollop of spiced sour cream that pairs perfectly with balsamic-kissed fruit.

Can of mandarin orange segments, drained	10 oz.	284 mL
Cubed cantaloupe (3/4 inch, 2 cm, pieces)	1 1/2 cups	375 mL
Halved green grapes	1 1/2 cups	375 mL
Sliced fresh strawberries	1 1/2 cups	375 mL
Balsamic vinegar	2 tsp.	10 mL
Granulated sugar	2 tsp.	10 mL
Sour cream	1/2 cup	125 mL
Granulated sugar	1 tbsp.	15 mL
Ground cinnamon	1/8 tsp.	0.5 mL
Ground cloves, sprinkle		
Salt, sprinkle		

Combine first 6 ingredients in large bowl. Let stand, covered, in refrigerator for 1 hour, stirring occasionally. Transfer to 6 serving bowls.

Combine remaining 5 ingredients in small bowl. Spoon over fruit mixture. Serves 6.

1 serving: 121 Calories; 3.6 g Total Fat (trace Mono, 0.1 g Poly, 2.4 g Sat); 13 mg Cholesterol; 21 g Carbohydrate; 2 g Fibre; 2 g Protein; 17 mg Sodium

Turkey Wild Rice Soup

For the heartiest turkey soup, try this big-batch version that's loaded with wild rice and veggies. This will store in an airtight container in the freezer for up to three months. You can use the leftover turkey meat and bones from Wild Rice-Stuffed Turkey, page 86.

Leftover turkey carcass	1	1
Water	20 cups	5 L
Celery ribs, halved	2	2
Large carrots, halved	2	2
Medium onion (unpeeled), halved	1	1
Bay leaves	2	2
Dried thyme	1 tsp.	5 mL
Cooking oil	1 tbsp.	15 mL
Chopped onion	1 cup	250 mL
Garlic cloves, minced	2	2
(or 1/2 tsp., 2 mL, powder)		
Sliced carrot	1 cup	250 mL
Sliced celery	1 cup	250 mL
Wild rice	1/2 cup	125 mL
Dried sage	1 tsp.	5 mL
Dried thyme	1/2 tsp	2 mL
Salt	1 1/2 tsp.	7 mL
Pepper	1/2 tsp.	2 mL
Chopped fresh spinach leaves, lightly packed	3 cups	750 mL
Chopped cooked turkey (see Note 1)	2 cups	500 mL

Break up turkey carcass to fit in large pot. Add water. Bring to a boil. Boil, uncovered, for 5 minutes without stirring. Skim and discard foam.

Add next 5 ingredients. Stir. Reduce heat to medium-low. Simmer, partially covered, for about 3 hours until meat falls off bones. Remove from heat. Discard larger bones. Strain stock through sieve into extra-large bowl. Discard solids. Skim and discard fat (see Note 2).

Heat cooking oil in Dutch oven on medium. Add onion and garlic. Cook for about 5 minutes, stirring often, until onion is softened.

(continued on next page)

Add next 7 ingredients and stock. Stir. Bring to a boil. Reduce heat to medium-low. Simmer, partially covered, for about 1 hour until rice is tender.

Add spinach and turkey. Cook for about 3 minutes, stirring occasionally, until heated through. Makes about 13 cups (3.25 L).

1 cup (250 mL): 84 Calories; 2.3 g Total Fat (0.9 g Mono, 0.7 g Poly, 0.5 g Sat); 16 mg Cholesterol; 8 g Carbohydrate; 1 g Fibre; 8 g Protein; 304 mg Sodium

Note 1: Don't have any leftover turkey? Start with 1 boneless, skinless turkey breast (about 10 oz., 285 g). Place in large frying pan with 1 cup (250 mL) water or chicken broth. Simmer, covered, for 12 to 14 minutes until no longer pink inside. Drain. Chop. Makes about 2 cups (500 mL).

Note 2: To reduce the fat content of the soup, chill the broth in the refrigerator. The fat will harden on the surface, making it easy to lift out.

Spiced Carrot Bisque

A thick and warming soup with a gentle spicy heat and creamy chai flavour. This slow-cooked soup will store in an airtight container in the freezer for up to three months.

Prepared chicken broth	4 1/2 cups	1.1 L
Sliced carrot	3 cups	750 mL
Chai tea concentrate	1 cup	250 mL
Chopped onion	1 cup	250 mL
Chopped celery	1/2 cup	125 mL
Long-grain brown (or white) rice	1/2 cup	125 mL
Garlic clove, minced	1	1
(or 1/4 tsp., 1 mL, powder)		
Dried crushed chilies	1/8 tsp.	0.5 mL
Milk	1/2 cup	125 mL

Combine first 8 ingredients in 3 1/2 to 4 quart (3.5 to 4 L) slow cooker. Cook, covered, on Low for 7 to 8 hours or on High for 3 1/2 to 4 hours. Carefully process with hand blender or in blender in batches until smooth (see Safety Tip).

Add milk. Stir. Makes about 8 cups (2 L).

1 cup (250 mL): 109 Calories; 1.4 g Total Fat (0.5 g Mono, 0.4 g Poly, 0.4 g Sat); 1 mg Cholesterol; 21 g Carbohydrate; 2 g Fibre; 5 g Protein; 486 mg Sodium

Safety Tip: Follow manufacturer's instructions for processing hot liquids.

Cranberry Confetti Slaw

This cheery veggie slaw will brighten up the table. It's fresh and very crisp with soft cranberry bites and a sweet vinaigrette.

Julienned zucchini (with peel), see Note	1 1/2 cups	375 mL
Bag of broccoli slaw (or shredded cabbage with carrot)	12 oz.	340 g
Slivered green pepper	1/2 cup	125 mL
Slivered red pepper	1/2 cup	125 mL
Dried cranberries	1/4 cup	60 mL
Julienned radish (see Note)	1/4 cup	60 mL
Thinly sliced green onion	1/4 cup	60 mL
Cooking oil	1/4 cup	60 mL
Frozen concentrated cranberry cocktail, thawed	1/4 cup	60 mL
Raspberry vinegar	2 tbsp.	30 mL
Dijon mustard	1 tsp.	5 mL
Granulated sugar	1 tsp.	5 mL
Salt	1/2 tsp.	2 mL
Pepper	1/4 tsp.	1 mL

Toss first 7 ingredients in large bowl.

Whisk remaining 7 ingredients in small bowl until smooth. Drizzle over slaw. Toss. Makes about 8 1/2 cups (2.1 L).

1 cup (250 mL): 110 Calories; 6.7 g Total Fat (3.9 g Mono, 2.0 g Poly, 0.5 g Sat); 0 mg Cholesterol; 13 g Carbohydrate; 2 g Fibre; 1 g Protein; 161 mg Sodium

Pictured on page 89.

Note: To julienne, cut into very thin strips that resemble matchsticks.

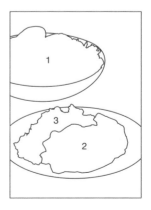

1. Bacon and Honey Spinach Salad, page 55
2. Coq au Vin Blanc, page 92
3. Creamy Roasted Garlic Potatoes, page 112

Props: Pier 1

Bacon and Honey Spinach Salad

A sweet and pleasing blend of fresh and flavourful ingredients—juicy pieces of mandarin and green apple complement salty bacon.

Bacon slices, chopped	6	6
Mayonnaise	1/4 cup	60 mL
Liquid honey	2 tbsp.	30 mL
Apple cider vinegar	1 tbsp.	15 mL
Salt, just a pinch		
Fresh spinach leaves, lightly packed	6 cups	1.5 L
Spring mix lettuce, lightly packed	2 cups	500 mL
Can of mandarin orange segments, drained	10 oz.	284 mL
Sliced unpeeled tart apple (such as Granny Smith)	1 cup	250 mL
Sliced natural almonds, toasted (see Tip, page 99)	1/2 cup	125 mL

Cook bacon in large frying pan on medium until crisp. Transfer with slotted spoon to paper towel-lined plate to drain.

Combine next 4 ingredients in small bowl. Add bacon. Stir.

Toss remaining 5 ingredients in large bowl. Add mayonnaise mixture. Toss. Makes about 8 cups (2 L).

1 cup (250 mL): 159 Calories; 10.8 g Total Fat (2.8 g Mono, 1.0 g Poly, 1.7 g Sat); 8 mg Cholesterol; 14 g Carbohydrate; 3 g Fibre; 4 g Protein; 167 mg Sodium

Pictured on page 53.

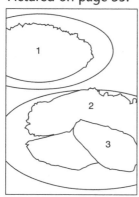

1. Curry Vegetable Pilaf, page 97
2. Parmesan Pear Salad, page 59
3. Mushroom Risotto Parcels, page 98

Spanish Lentil Spinach Soup

Here is a healthy vegetarian offering to serve up during the holidays. This thick, hearty soup is pleasantly flavoured with cumin and gets its texture from lentils and vegetables. It stores well in an airtight container in the freezer for up to three months.

Cooking oil	1 tbsp.	15 mL
Chopped onion	1 1/2 cups	375 mL
Diced carrot	1 cup	250 mL
Diced peeled potato	1 cup	250 mL
Diced red pepper	1 cup	250 mL
Smoked (sweet) paprika	1 1/2 tsp.	7 mL
Ground cumin	1 tsp.	5 mL
Garlic cloves, minced	2	2
(or 1/2 tsp., 2 mL, powder)		
Pepper	1/2 tsp	2 mL
Prepared vegetable broth	4 cups	1 L
Water	2 cups	500 mL
Dried green lentils	1 1/2 cups	375 mL
Bay leaf	1	1
Chopped fresh spinach leaves, lightly packed	2 cups	500 mL
Chopped tomato	1 cup	250 mL
Red wine vinegar	2 tbsp.	30 mL
Granulated sugar	1/2 tsp.	2 mL

Heat cooking oil in large saucepan on medium. Add onion. Cook for about 8 minutes, stirring often, until softened.

Add next 7 ingredients. Stir. Cook for about 3 minutes, stirring often, until garlic is fragrant.

Add next 4 ingredients. Heat and stir, scraping any brown bits from bottom of pan, until boiling. Reduce heat to medium-low. Simmer, partially covered, for about 45 minutes, stirring occasionally, until lentils are tender. Remove and discard bay leaf.

Add remaining 4 ingredients. Heat and stir for about 2 minutes until spinach is wilted. Makes about 9 1/4 cups (2.3 L).

1 cup (250 mL): 164 Calories; 2.7 g Total Fat (0.9 g Mono, 0.6 g Poly, 0.2 g Sat); 0 mg Cholesterol; 29 g Carbohydrate; 7 g Fibre; 8 g Protein; 220 mg Sodium

Salads & Soups

Roasted Butternut Soup

A smooth squash soup with a gorgeous colour and a hint of ginger—this would look lovely served in bowls of a contrasting colour, such as purple or turquoise. It will store in an airtight container in the freezer for up to three months.

Chopped butternut squash	8 cups	2 L
Cooking oil	2 tbsp.	30 mL
Salt	1/2 tsp.	2 mL
Cooking oil	1 tbsp.	15 mL
Chopped onion	1 cup	250 mL
Chopped peeled cooking apple (such as McIntosh)	2 cups	500 mL
Prepared chicken broth	4 cups	1 L
Finely grated ginger root (or 1/2 tsp., 2 mL, ground ginger)	2 tsp.	10 mL
Pepper	1/8 tsp.	0.5 mL
Milk	2 cups	500 mL

Toss first 3 ingredients in extra-large bowl. Arrange in single layer on greased baking sheet with sides. Cook in 400°F (205°C) oven for about 30 minutes, stirring at halftime, until tender and starting to brown.

Heat second amount of cooking oil in Dutch oven on medium. Add onion. Cook for about 5 minutes, stirring often, until onion is softened.

Add apple. Cook for about 5 minutes, stirring occasionally, until apple is softened.

Add next 3 ingredients and squash. Bring to a boil. Boil gently, uncovered, for 10 minutes to blend flavours. Carefully process with hand blender or in blender in batches until smooth (see Safety Tip). Return to same pot.

Add milk. Stir. Makes about 9 3/4 cups (2.4 L).

1 cup (250 mL): 186 Calories; 5.7 g Total Fat (3.0 g Mono, 1.5 g Poly, 0.8 g Sat); 3 mg Cholesterol; 31 g Carbohydrate; 5 g Fibre; 6 g Protein; 473 mg Sodium

Pictured on page 36.

Safety Tip: Follow manufacturer's instructions for processing hot liquids.

Roasted Borscht

A classic, vibrantly coloured borscht with lots of dill flavour and a nice texture. Stir in buttermilk at the end for added creaminess. An excellent choice to serve as one of the twelve meatless dishes for Ukrainian Christmas Eve!

Chopped peeled beets (see Note)	3 cups	750 mL
Chopped carrot	1 cup	250 mL
Cooking oil	2 tsp.	10 mL
Salt, sprinkle		
Pepper, sprinkle		
Cooking oil	2 tsp.	10 mL
Chopped onion	1 cup	250 mL
Diced peeled cooking apple	1 cup	250 mL
(such as McIntosh)		
Diced celery	1/2 cup	125 mL
Garlic clove, minced	1	1
(or 1/4 tsp., 1 mL, powder)		
Prepared vegetable broth	6 cups	1.5 L
Bay leaf	1	1
Salt	1/2 tsp.	2 mL
Pepper	1/4 tsp.	1 mL
Sprig of fresh thyme	1	1
(or 1/8 tsp., 0.5 mL, dried)		
Chopped fresh dill	2 tbsp.	30 mL
(or 1 1/2 tsp., 7 mL, dried)		
Lemon juice	2 tsp.	10 mL

Toss first 5 ingredients in large bowl. Transfer to 16 x 16 inch (40 x 40 cm) piece of heavy-duty (or double layer of regular) foil. Fold edges of foil together over beet mixture to enclose. Fold ends to seal completely. Place, seam-side up, on baking sheet with sides. Cook in 425°F (220°C) oven for about 45 minutes until tender. Let stand until cool enough to handle.

Heat second amount of cooking oil in large saucepan on medium. Add next 4 ingredients. Cook for about 10 minutes, stirring often, until onion is softened.

(continued on next page)

Salads & Soups

Add next 5 ingredients and beet mixture. Bring to a boil. Reduce heat to medium-low. Simmer, covered, for 30 minutes. Remove and discard bay leaf and thyme sprig. Carefully process with hand blender or in blender in batches until almost smooth (see Safety Tip).

Add dill and lemon juice. Stir. Makes about 7 1/2 cups (1.9 L).

1 cup (250 mL): 96 Calories; 3.1 g Total Fat (1.5 g Mono, 0.8 g Poly, 0.2 g Sat); 0 mg Cholesterol; 16 g Carbohydrate; 4 g Fibre; 2 g Protein; 585 mg Sodium

Note: Don't get caught red-handed! Wear rubber gloves when handling beets.

Safety Tip: Follow manufacturer's instructions for processing hot liquids.

Parmesan Pear Salad

A delectable combination of juicy pears with occasional bits of pecans and ginger. Shaved Parmesan makes for a deliciously savoury contrast in an overall sweet salad. Use fresh rather than pre-packaged Parmesan for the best flavour.

Olive (or cooking) oil	3 tbsp.	50 mL
Ginger marmalade, warmed	2 tbsp.	30 mL
White balsamic (or white wine) vinegar	2 tbsp.	30 mL
Pepper	1/4 tsp.	1 mL
Mixed salad greens, lightly packed	6 cups	1.5 L
Arugula, lightly packed	2 cups	500 mL
Thinly sliced peeled pear	1 cup	250 mL
Shaved Parmesan cheese	1/2 cup	125 mL
Chopped pecans, toasted (see Tip, page 99)	1/4 cup	60 mL

Whisk first 4 ingredients in large bowl. Add next 3 ingredients. Toss.

Scatter cheese and pecans over top. Makes about 8 1/2 cups (2.1 L).

1 cup (250 mL): 129 Calories; 9.5 g Total Fat (4.4 g Mono, 2.3 g Poly, 1.5 g Sat); 5 mg Cholesterol; 8 g Carbohydrate; 2 g Fibre; 4 g Protein; 128 mg Sodium

Pictured on page 54.

Cranberry Waldorf Jellied Salad

*Inspired by the famed Waldorf salad, this festively coloured jelly version
is filled with green apple, pecans and cranberries. This salad must be
prepared several hours in advance, but it can easily be made the night
before your big event.*

Box of lime jelly powder (gelatin)	3 oz.	85 g
Granulated sugar	1/4 cup	60 mL
Boiling water	1 cup	250 mL
Cold water	1/2 cup	125 mL
Chopped frozen cranberries	1 cup	250 mL
Diced celery	1/2 cup	125 mL
Finely chopped unpeeled tart apple (such as Granny Smith)	1/2 cup	125 mL
Finely chopped pecans, toasted (see Tip, page 99)	1/4 cup	60 mL
Sour cream	1/4 cup	60 mL
Whipping cream	1 cup	250 mL

Put jelly powder and sugar into medium heatproof bowl. Pour boiling
water over top. Stir until jelly powder is dissolved.

Add cold water. Stir. Chill for about 1 hour, stirring occasionally, until
mixture thickens to syrup consistency.

Add next 5 ingredients. Stir gently.

Beat whipping cream in medium bowl until stiff peaks form. Fold into
cranberry mixture until no white streaks remain. Pour into greased 6 cup
(1.5 L) mold or serving bowl. Chill, covered, for at least 6 hours or
overnight until firm. Loosen salad in mold. Invert onto serving plate. Makes
about 5 1/2 cups (1.4 L).

*1 cup (250 mL): 303 Calories; 21.8 g Total Fat (6.8 g Mono, 1.8 g Poly, 11.6 g Sat);
67 mg Cholesterol; 27 g Carbohydrate; 2 g Fibre; 3 g Protein; 100 mg Sodium*

Salads & Soups

Cranberry Pot Roast

This hearty pot roast, easy to make in your slow cooker, includes a gravy with a touch of cranberry sweetness. Use any leftover beef to make Stuffed Yorkshire Puddings, page 12. This recipe can also be made in advance and reheated just before the guests are due to arrive.

Sliced onion	2 cups	500 mL
Bay leaves	2	2
Boneless beef cross-rib roast	5 lbs.	2.3 kg
Prepared beef broth	1 cup	250 mL
Whole cranberry sauce	1 cup	250 mL
Soy sauce	1/3 cup	75 mL
Minute tapioca	2 tbsp.	30 mL

Place first 3 ingredients, in order given, in 4 to 5 quart (4 to 5 L) slow cooker.

Combine remaining 4 ingredients in small bowl. Pour over roast. Cook, covered, on High for 4 to 5 hours. Transfer roast to cutting board. Cover with foil. Let stand for 10 minutes. Skim and discard fat from cooking liquid. Remove and discard bay leaves. Carefully process with hand blender or in blender in batches until smooth (see Safety Tip). Slice roast and arrange on large serving plate. Serve with onion mixture (see Note). Serves 12.

1 serving: 407 Calories; 14.6 g Total Fat (6.2 g Mono, 0.6 g Poly, 5.3 g Sat); 163 mg Cholesterol; 13 g Carbohydrate; 1 g Fibre; 53 g Protein; 754 mg Sodium

Safety Tip: Follow manufacturer's instructions for processing hot liquids.

Note: To make ahead and serve the next day, let roast stand until cool. Cut into slices and arrange in 9 x 13 inch (23 x 33 cm) baking dish. Pour onion mixture over top. Chill, covered, until ready to reheat. Bake, covered, in 350°F (175°C) oven for 60 to 70 minutes until internal temperature of beef mixture reaches 165°F (74°C).

Paré Pointer
If you find someone's work speaks for itself, don't interrupt.

Italian Beef Shells

These pasta shells are filled to the brim with a mildly seasoned beef mixture and topped with crisp golden crumbs.

Prepared beef broth	1 3/4 cups	425 mL
Can of tomato sauce	14 oz.	398 mL
Water	12 cups	3 L
Salt	1 1/2 tsp.	7 mL
Jumbo shell pasta	28	28
Large egg	1	1
Finely chopped onion	3/4 cup	175 mL
Jar of marinated artichokes, drained and finely chopped	6 oz.	170 mL
Fine dry bread crumbs	1/2 cup	125 mL
Milk	1/2 cup	125 mL
Chopped fresh basil (or 1 1/2 tsp., 7 mL, dried)	2 tbsp.	30 mL
Balsamic vinegar	1 tbsp.	15 mL
Dried oregano	1/2 tsp.	2 mL
Garlic clove, minced (or 1/4 tsp., 1 mL, powder)	1	1
Salt	1/4 tsp.	1 mL
Pepper	1/8 tsp.	0.5 mL
Lean ground beef ·	1 lb.	454 g
Crushed round butter-flavoured crackers (about 30 crackers)	1 cup	250 mL
Grated Parmesan cheese	1/4 cup	60 mL

Chopped fresh parsley, for garnish

Combine broth and tomato sauce in 9 x 13 inch (23 x 33 cm) baking dish.

Combine water and salt in Dutch oven. Bring to a boil. Add pasta. Boil, uncovered, for 10 to 12 minutes, stirring occasionally, until tender but firm. Drain.

(continued on next page)

Combine next 11 ingredients in large bowl.

Add beef. Mix well. Spoon about 2 tbsp. (30 mL) beef mixture into each pasta shell. Arrange in single layer over broth mixture. Cook, covered, in 350°F (175°C) oven for 1 hour.

Combine crushed crackers and cheese in small bowl. Sprinkle over shells. Cook, uncovered, for about 15 minutes until crushed crackers are browned and internal temperature of filling reaches 160°F (71°C).

Sprinkle with parsley. Makes 28 stuffed shells. Serves 4.

1 serving: 703 Calories; 22.9 g Total Fat (9.6 g Mono, 0.9 g Poly, 7.8 g Sat); 137 mg Cholesterol; 79 g Carbohydrate; 4 g Fibre; 42 g Protein; 1942 mg Sodium

Pictured on page 71.

Paré Pointer

The reason bagpipers walk fast when they play is to try and get away from the noise.

Take-the-Chill-Off Chili

Warm up with this chili after a day on the slopes or the ice rink! This substantial batch of chili is a great make-ahead option for serving a crowd, and can be frozen in airtight containers for up to three months.

Cooking oil	1 tbsp.	15 mL
Beef blade steak, cut into	1 1/2 lbs.	680 g
1/2 inch (12 mm) pieces		
Sliced fresh white mushrooms	2 cups	500 mL
Chopped carrot	1 1/2 cups	375 mL
Chopped celery	1 cup	250 mL
Chopped onion	1 cup	250 mL
Garlic cloves, minced	2	2
(or 1/2 tsp., 2 mL, powder)		
Can of diced tomatoes (with juice)	28 oz.	796 mL
Can of black beans, rinsed and drained	19 oz.	540 mL
Can of mixed beans, rinsed and drained	19 oz.	540 mL
Frozen kernel corn	1 cup	250 mL
Can of tomato sauce	7 1/2 oz.	213 mL
Can of diced green chilies	4 oz.	113 g
Chili powder	2 tbsp.	30 mL
Cocoa, sifted if lumpy	1 tbsp.	15 mL
Ground cumin	2 tsp.	10 mL
Smoked (sweet) paprika	1 1/2 tsp.	7 mL
Granulated sugar	1 tsp.	5 mL
Cayenne pepper	1/2 tsp.	2 mL
Salt	1/2 tsp.	2 mL
Chopped red pepper	1 1/2 cups	375 mL

Heat cooking oil in Dutch oven on medium-high. Add beef. Cook for about 10 minutes, stirring occasionally, until browned. Transfer to large plate. Reduce heat to medium.

Add next 5 ingredients to same pot. Cook for about 10 minutes, stirring often, until onion is softened.

Add next 13 ingredients and beef. Stir. Bring to a boil. Reduce heat to medium-low. Simmer, covered, for 30 minutes.

(continued on next page)

Main Courses - Beef

Add red pepper. Stir. Simmer, covered, for about 50 minutes, stirring occasionally, until beef is tender. Makes about 12 cups (4 L).

1 cup (250 mL): 240 Calories; 8.1 g Total Fat (3.1 g Mono, 1.1 g Poly, 2.4 g Sat); 37 mg Cholesterol; 24 g Carbohydrate; 7 g Fibre; 18 g Protein; 636 mg Sodium

Garlic Herb-Crusted Steaks

Delicious steaks with a crisp, seasoned topping and tasty Dijon flavour. This special steak dinner is ideal for winter days since it requires the oven.

Cooking oil	2 tsp.	10 mL
Beef rib-eye steak, cut into 4 equal portions	1 lb.	454 g
Salt, sprinkle		
Pepper	1/2 tsp.	2 mL
Fresh bread crumbs	1 cup	250 mL
Grated onion	2 tbsp.	30 mL
Chopped fresh rosemary (or 1/4 tsp., 1 mL, dried, crushed)	1 tsp.	5 mL
Chopped fresh thyme (or 1/4 tsp., 1 mL, dried)	1 tsp.	5 mL
Garlic cloves, minced (or 1/2 tsp., 2 mL, powder)	2	2
Butter (or hard margarine), melted	2 tbsp.	30 mL
Dijon mustard	4 tsp.	20 mL

Heat cooking oil in large frying pan on medium-high. Sprinkle both sides of steaks with salt and pepper. Add to frying pan. Cook for about 2 minutes per side until browned. Transfer to greased wire rack set in large baking sheet with sides. Let stand for 5 minutes.

Combine next 5 ingredients in small bowl. Drizzle with butter. Toss.

Brush tops of steaks with mustard. Press bread crumb mixture onto mustard. Cook on centre rack in 400°F (205°C) oven for about 15 minutes until internal temperature reaches 160°F (71°C) for medium or until steaks reach desired doneness. Cover loosely with foil. Let stand for 10 minutes. Serves 4.

1 serving: 401 Calories; 23.1 g Total Fat (8.4 g Mono, 1.4 g Poly, 9.0 g Sat); 117 mg Cholesterol; 20 g Carbohydrate; 1 g Fibre; 26 g Protein; 359 mg Sodium

Pictured on page 71.

Greek Beef Strudel

A unique and intriguing main course option, this attractive phyllo roll cuts into neat slices. The moist, flavourful filling of ground beef, spinach and feta is infused with lemon and oregano.

Olive (or cooking) oil	1 tsp.	5 mL
Lean ground beef	1 lb.	454 g
Finely chopped onion	1/4 cup	60 mL
Dried oregano	1 tsp.	5 mL
Garlic cloves, minced	2	2
(or 1/2 tsp., 2 mL, powder)		
Salt	1/4 tsp.	1 mL
Pepper	1/4 tsp.	1 mL
Large egg, fork-beaten	1	1
Box of frozen chopped spinach, thawed and squeezed dry	10 oz.	300 g
Crumbled feta cheese	3/4 cup	175 mL
Finely chopped roasted red peppers	1/4 cup	60 mL
Fine dry bread crumbs	2 tbsp.	30 mL
Grated lemon zest	1 tsp.	5 mL
Frozen phyllo pastry sheets, thawed according to package directions	8	8
Butter (or hard margarine), melted	1/3 cup	75 mL

Heat olive oil in large frying pan on medium-high. Add beef. Scramble-fry for about 5 minutes until starting to brown.

Add next 5 ingredients. Cook on medium for about 4 minutes, stirring often, until onion is softened and oregano is fragrant. Transfer to large bowl. Cool.

Add next 6 ingredients. Mix well.

Lay tea towel on work surface, short end closest to you. Place 1 pastry sheet on towel, lining up short end of pastry sheet with short end of towel. Cover remaining sheets with damp towel to prevent drying. Place second sheet at far end of first sheet with 6 inches (15 cm) overlapping in the middle.

(continued on next page)

Brush with butter. Repeat, layering with remaining sheets and butter. Spoon ground beef mixture onto pastry, 6 inches (15 cm) from closest edge. Bring pastry up over filling. Roll up tightly to enclose filling, using tea towel as guide. Leave ends open. Pack any loose filling back into roll. Place, seam-side down, on greased baking sheet with sides. Brush with remaining butter. Bake in 375°F (190°C) oven for about 35 minutes until pastry is golden. Cuts into 8 slices.

1 slice: 326 Calories; 21.5 g Total Fat (3.8 g Mono, 0.8 g Poly, 10.8 g Sat); 98 mg Cholesterol; 15 g Carbohydrate; 1 g Fibre; 17 g Protein; 591 mg Sodium

Pictured on page 71.

Paré Pointer

After seeing the bread box, the milk shake and the ginger snap, the bananas split.

Tourtière

Tourtière is a meat pie traditionally served in French Canadian homes during the holidays. This version features beef and pork seasoned with fragrant allspice and cloves.

Cooking oil	1 tsp.	5 mL
Finely chopped onion	1 cup	250 mL
Garlic cloves, minced	2	2
(or 1/2 tsp., 2 mL, powder)		
Lean ground beef	1/2 lb.	225 g
Lean ground pork	1/2 lb.	225 g
Water	1/2 cup	125 mL
Ground allspice	1/4 tsp.	1 mL
Salt	1/4 tsp.	1 mL
Pepper	1/8 tsp.	0.5 mL
Ground cloves	1/8 tsp.	0.5 mL
Fine dry bread crumbs	1/2 cup	125 mL
Pastry for 2 crust 9 inch (23 cm) pie		
Large egg, fork-beaten	1	1

Heat cooking oil in large saucepan on medium. Add onion. Cook for about 5 minutes, stirring often, until softened.

Add garlic. Heat and stir for about 1 minute until fragrant.

Add next 7 ingredients. Stir. Bring to a boil. Boil gently, uncovered, for about 20 minutes, stirring occasionally, until liquid is reduced by half. Remove from heat.

Add bread crumbs. Mix well. Cool.

Divide pastry into 2 portions, making 1 portion slightly larger than the other. Shape each portion into slightly flattened disc. Roll out larger portion on lightly floured surface to about 1/8 inch (3 mm) thickness. Line 9 inch (23 cm) pie plate. Spread beef mixture evenly in shell. Roll out smaller portion on lightly floured surface to about 1/8 inch (3 mm) thickness. Dampen edge of pastry shell with water. Cover with remaining pastry. Trim and crimp decorative edge to seal.

(continued on next page)

Brush with egg. Cut several vents in top to allow steam to escape. Bake on bottom rack in 375°F (190°C) oven for about 1 hour until pastry is golden brown. Let stand on wire rack for 15 minutes. Cuts into 8 wedges.

1 wedge: 413 Calories; 24.1 g Total Fat (2.5 g Mono, 0.7 g Poly, 9.5 g Sat); 75 mg Cholesterol; 33 g Carbohydrate; 1 g Fibre; 15 g Protein; 368 mg Sodium

Thyme-Roasted Tenderloin

A beautiful roast to serve at an extra-special dinner party—everyone will love the fresh thyme and garlic flavour. Look for a centre-cut roast for uniform cooking.

Beef tenderloin roast	2 1/2 lbs.	1.1 kg
Montreal steak spice	1/2 tsp.	2 mL
Cooking oil	2 tbsp.	30 mL
Butter (or hard margarine), softened	1 tbsp.	15 mL
Chopped fresh thyme	1 tsp.	5 mL
(or 1/4 tsp., 1 mL, dried)		
Dry mustard	1 tsp.	5 mL
Coarsely ground pepper	1/2 tsp.	2 mL
Garlic cloves, minced	2	2
(or 1/2 tsp., 2 mL, powder)		
Grated lemon zest	1/2 tsp.	2 mL

Sprinkle roast with steak spice. Heat cooking oil in large frying pan on medium-high. Add roast. Cook for about 5 minutes, turning occasionally, until browned on all sides. Place on greased wire rack set in large baking sheet with sides.

Combine remaining 6 ingredients in small bowl. Brush over roast. Cook in 350°F (175°C) oven for 40 to 45 minutes until internal temperature reaches 160°F (71°C) for medium or until roast reaches desired doneness. Transfer to cutting board. Cover with foil. Let stand for 10 minutes. Slice thinly. Serves 8.

1 serving: 197 Calories; 10.0 g Total Fat (4.3 g Mono, 1.1 g Poly, 3.0 g Sat); 79 mg Cholesterol; 1 g Carbohydrate; trace Fibre; 28 g Protein; 122 mg Sodium

Festive Fish Parcels

A refreshingly light option for your holiday main course. Freshly flavoured with dill and lemon, firm haddock is paired with pretty red pepper and green onion strips.

Haddock fillets, any small bones removed	1 lb.	454 g
Cooking oil	1 tbsp.	15 mL
Chopped fresh dill	1 tsp.	5 mL
(or 1/4 tsp., 1 mL, dried)		
Grated lemon zest	1/4 tsp.	1 mL
Salt	1/8 tsp.	0.5 mL
Pepper	1/8 tsp.	0.5 mL
Thin red pepper slices, halved	6	6
Green onions (green part only),	4	4
cut into 3 pieces each		

Cut 4 sheets of parchment paper, about 15 inches (38 cm) long. Arrange fillets in centre of each sheet.

Combine next 5 ingredients in small cup. Spread over fillets.

Arrange red pepper and green onion over top. Bring edges of parchment paper together over seafood to enclose. Fold ends together several times to seal completely. Arrange on baking sheet with sides. Cook in 400°F (205°C) oven for about 12 minutes until fish flakes easily when tested with fork. Makes 4 parcels.

1 parcel: 134 Calories; 4.3 g Total Fat (2.2 g Mono, 1.3 g Poly, 0.4 g Sat); 65 mg Cholesterol; 1 g Carbohydrate; 1 g Fibre; 22 g Protein; 150 mg Sodium

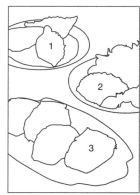

1. Italian Beef Shells, page 62
2. Garlic Herb-Crusted Steaks, page 65
3. Greek Beef Strudel, page 66

Honey Cajun Salmon

Baked salmon with an appetizing and colourful Cajun spice coating. Serve with fresh lemon wedges—a squeeze will bring out the subtle honey sweetness.

Liquid honey	1/3 cup	75 mL
Gin	2 tbsp.	30 mL
Lemon juice	1 tbsp.	15 mL
Salmon fillet	2 lbs.	900 g
Cajun seasoning	3 tbsp.	50 mL

Combine first 3 ingredients in small cup.

Place fillet on foil-lined baking sheet with sides. Brush with 1/4 cup (60 mL) honey mixture.

Sprinkle with Cajun seasoning. Cook in 350°F (175°C) oven for about 30 minutes until fish flakes easily when tested with fork. Drizzle with remaining honey mixture. Serves 8.

1 serving: 215 Calories; 7.2 g Total Fat (2.4 g Mono, 2.9 g Poly, 1.1 g Sat); 62 mg Cholesterol; 11 g Carbohydrate; trace Fibre; 23 g Protein; 658 mg Sodium

Pictured on page 36.

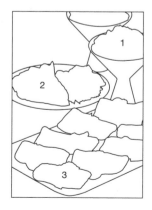

1. Granola Parfaits, page 46
2. Crab and Red Pepper Quiche, page 45
3. Cranberry Orange Blintzes, page 48

Props: Le Gnome
      Ikea

Seafood Gratin

This gratin's inviting browned-panko topping makes you want to dig in.
Beneath, you'll find tender, delicate seafood in a light sauce with plenty
of dill and thyme.

Halibut fillets, any small bones removed, cut into 3/4 inch (2 cm) pieces	3/4 lb.	340 g
Small bay scallops	1/2 lb.	225 g
Uncooked medium shrimp (peeled and deveined)	1/2 lb.	225 g
Butter (or hard margarine)	1 tbsp.	15 mL
Sliced leek (white part only)	1 cup	250 mL
Finely chopped carrot	1/3 cup	75 mL
Finely chopped celery	1/3 cup	75 mL
Butter (or hard margarine)	2 tbsp.	30 mL
All-purpose flour	3 tbsp.	50 mL
Dried dillweed	1 tsp.	5 mL
Dried thyme	1/2 tsp.	2 mL
Salt	1/2 tsp.	2 mL
Pepper	1/4 tsp.	1 mL
Milk	1 1/4 cups	300 mL
Panko (or fine dry) bread crumbs	1 cup	250 mL
Grated Parmesan cheese	2 tbsp.	30 mL
Butter (or hard margarine), melted	1 tbsp.	15 mL

Pour water into large frying pan until about 1 inch (2.5 cm) deep. Bring to a boil. Add first 3 ingredients. Cook, uncovered, for 2 minutes. Drain, reserving 1 cup (250 mL) cooking liquid. Scatter fish mixture in greased shallow 2 quart (2 L) casserole.

Melt first amount of butter in large frying pan on medium. Add next 3 ingredients. Cook for about 8 minutes, stirring often, until vegetables are softened. Scatter over seafood mixture.

Melt second amount of butter in same frying pan. Add next 5 ingredients. Heat and stir for 1 minute. Slowly add reserved cooking liquid, stirring constantly until smooth.

(continued on next page)

Add milk. Heat and stir for about 3 minutes until boiling and thickened. Pour over seafood mixture.

Combine remaining 3 ingredients in small bowl. Sprinkle over top. Bake in 375°F (190°C) oven for about 20 minutes until golden. Serves 6.

1 serving: 328 Calories; 11.1 g Total Fat (2.7 g Mono, 1.1 g Poly, 5.8 g Sat); 113 mg Cholesterol; 24 g Carbohydrate; 1 g Fibre; 31 g Protein; 507 mg Sodium

 To devein shrimp, strip off legs and peel off shell. Using a small, sharp knife, make a shallow cut along the centre of back. Rinse under cold water to wash out the dark vein.

Trout and Pea Risotto

Delicate colours and flavours are well-matched in this creamy risotto with hints of lemon and Parmesan—an elegant main course fit for a dinner party.

Prepared vegetable broth	5 cups	1.25 L
Olive (or cooking) oil	1 tbsp.	15 mL
Diced fennel bulb (white part only)	1 1/2 cups	375 mL
Diced onion	1 cup	250 mL
Arborio rice	1 1/2 cups	375 mL
Garlic clove, minced	1	1
(or 1/4 tsp., 1 mL, powder)		
Dry (or alcohol-free) white wine	1/2 cup	125 mL
Frozen tiny peas, thawed	2 cups	500 mL
Rainbow trout fillets, any small bones removed	3/4 lb.	340 g
Salt, sprinkle		
Pepper, sprinkle		
Butter (or hard margarine)	1 tbsp.	15 mL
Grated Parmesan cheese	1/2 cup	125 mL
Chopped fresh parsley	3 tbsp.	50 mL
(or 1 1/2 tsp., 7 mL, flakes)		
Lemon juice	3 tbsp.	50 mL
Coarsely ground pepper	1/2 tsp.	2 mL

Bring broth to a boil in small saucepan. Reduce heat to low. Cover to keep warm.

Heat olive oil in large saucepan on medium. Add fennel and onion. Cook for about 10 minutes, stirring often, until fennel and onion are softened.

Add rice and garlic. Heat and stir for about 1 minute until rice is coated and garlic is fragrant. Add wine. Heat and stir for about 1 minute until liquid is evaporated. Add 1 cup (250 mL) hot broth, stirring constantly until broth is absorbed. Repeat with remaining broth, 1 cup (250 mL) at a time, until broth is absorbed and rice is tender and creamy.

(continued on next page)

Add peas. Stir. Remove from heat. Cover to keep warm.

Sprinkle both sides of fillets with salt and pepper. Melt butter in large frying pan on medium. Add fillets. Cook for 1 to 2 minutes per side until fish flakes easily when tested with fork. Break into chunks.

Add remaining 4 ingredients and fish to rice mixture. Stir gently. Makes about 8 cups (2 L).

1 cup (250 mL): 251 Calories; 7.3 g Total Fat (1.9 g Mono, 1.1 g Poly, 2.4 g Sat); 34 mg Cholesterol 27 g Carbohydrate; 4 g Fibre; 16 g Protein; 509 mg Sodium

Paré Pointer

To avoid being irritated by biting insects, stop biting them.

Fig and Apple-Stuffed Pork

An attractive, spice-speckled pork roast stuffed with sweet apples and figs.

Butter (or hard margarine)	2 tbsp.	30 mL
Chopped onion	1/2 cup	125 mL
Chopped peeled tart apple (such as Granny Smith)	2 cups	500 mL
Chopped dried figs	1/2 cup	125 mL
Chopped fresh parsley (or 3/4 tsp., 4 mL, flakes)	1 tbsp.	15 mL
Chopped fresh thyme (or 3/4 tsp., 4 mL, dried)	1 tbsp.	15 mL
Unseasoned croutons (see Tip, page 113)	1 1/2 cups	375 mL
Salt	1/2 tsp.	2 mL
Pepper, just a pinch		
Prepared chicken broth	1/2 cup	125 mL
Boneless pork loin roast	3 lbs.	1.4 kg
Salt	1/2 tsp.	2 mL
Pepper	1 tsp.	5 mL

Heat butter in medium frying pan on medium. Add onion. Cook for about 5 minutes, stirring often, until softened.

Add next 4 ingredients. Cook for about 2 minutes, stirring occasionally, until apple starts to soften. Transfer to large bowl.

Add next 3 ingredients. Stir. Add broth, 1/4 cup (60 mL) at a time, stirring until croutons are moistened. Let stand for 10 minutes.

To butterfly roast, cut horizontally lengthwise almost, but not quite through to other side. Open flat. Spoon crouton mixture on 1 side of roast. Fold over to enclose filling. Tie with butcher's string. Sprinkle with second amount of salt and pepper. Place on greased wire rack set in medium roasting pan. Cook, uncovered, in 400°F (205°C) oven for about 30 minutes until starting to brown. Reduce heat to 325°F (160°C). Cook for about 45 minutes until internal temperature of pork (not stuffing) reaches 155°F (68°C). Transfer to cutting board. Cover with foil. Let stand for 10 minutes. Internal temperature of pork should rise to at least 160°F (71°C). Cut into 1/2 inch (12 mm) slices. Serves 8.

1 serving: 351 Calories; 14.9 g Total Fat (6.1 g Mono, 1.2 g Poly, 6.1 g Sat); 104 mg Cholesterol; 18 g Carbohydrate; 3 g Fibre; 36 g Protein; 470 mg Sodium

Pepper Pork Stew

A mild, saucy stew with moist pork and tender peppers—pair with your favourite stew accompaniment, from fresh bread to mashed potatoes, and serve for a casual family gathering.

Cooking oil	1 tbsp.	15 mL
Boneless pork shoulder blade steak, trimmed of fat and cut into 1 inch (2.5 cm) pieces	1 1/2 lbs.	680 g
Cooking oil	1 tsp.	5 mL
Sliced onion	1 cup	250 mL
Prepared chicken broth	1 1/2 cups	375 mL
Frozen concentrated orange juice, thawed	2 tbsp.	30 mL
Tomato paste (see Tip, page 93)	2 tbsp.	30 mL
Garlic cloves, thinly sliced	4	4
Dried thyme	1 tsp.	5 mL
Grated orange zest	1 tsp.	5 mL
Dried crushed chilies	1/4 tsp.	1 mL
Dried sage	1/4 tsp.	1 mL
Salt	1/2 tsp.	2 mL
Pepper	1/4 tsp.	1 mL
Thinly sliced green pepper	1 1/2 cups	375 mL
Thinly sliced red pepper	1 1/2 cups	375 mL

Heat first amount of cooking oil in Dutch oven on medium-high. Add pork. Cook for about 8 minutes, stirring often, until no longer pink. Transfer to plate. Reduce heat to medium.

Heat second amount of cooking oil in same pot. Add onion. Cook for about 5 minutes, stirring often, until softened.

Add next 10 ingredients and pork. Stir. Bring to a boil. Reduce heat to medium-low. Simmer, covered, for about 45 minutes, stirring occasionally, until pork is tender.

Add green and red pepper. Stir. Cook, covered, for about 15 minutes until pepper is tender. Makes about 5 1/2 cups (1.4 L).

1 cup (250 mL): 261 Calories; 11.7 g Total Fat (5.6 g Mono, 2.0 g Poly, 3.1 g Sat); 80 mg Cholesterol; 11 g Carbohydrate; 2 g Fibre; 27 g Protein; 532 mg Sodium

Pictured on page 90.

Ham With Sweet Cabbage

A traditional clove-studded ham is served with a colourful and rustic blend of cabbage, bacon and toasted hazelnuts. A warming meal for friends and family.

APPLE-GLAZED HAM

Apple jelly	1/2 cup	125 mL
Apple cider vinegar	2 tbsp.	30 mL
Partially cooked bone-in ham	8 lbs.	3.6 kg
Whole cloves, approximately	4 tsp.	20 mL

SAUTÉED SWEET CABBAGE

Orange juice	1/2 cup	125 mL
Apple cider vinegar	1/4 cup	60 mL
Brown sugar, packed	2 tbsp.	30 mL
Bacon slices, chopped	4	4
Shredded green cabbage, lightly packed	3 cups	750 mL
Shredded red cabbage, lightly packed	3 cups	750 mL
Thinly sliced onion	1 1/2 cups	375 mL
Chopped dried apricot	3/4 cup	175 mL
Salt	1/2 tsp.	2 mL
Pepper	1/8 tsp.	0.5 mL
Chopped hazelnuts (filberts), toasted (see Tip, page 99)	1/4 cup	60 mL
Sliced green onion	2 tbsp.	30 mL

Apple-Glazed Ham: Combine jelly and vinegar in small cup until smooth.

Using sharp knife, score ham in cross-hatch pattern, about 1/4 inch (6 mm) deep. Press whole clove into centre of each diamond shape. Place ham, fat-side up, on greased wire rack set in large roasting pan. Cook, uncovered, in 325°F (160°C) oven for 1 hour. Brush with jelly mixture. Cook, uncovered, for about 1 hour 45 minutes, brushing occasionally with remaining jelly mixture, until internal temperature reaches 160°F (71°C). Transfer to cutting board. Cover with foil. Let stand for 10 minutes. Slice thinly and arrange on large serving plate

(continued on next page)

Sautéed Sweet Cabbage: Combine first 3 ingredients in small cup. Set aside.

Cook bacon in large frying pan on medium until crisp. Transfer with slotted spoon to paper towel-lined plate to drain. Drain and discard all but 1 tbsp. (15 mL) drippings.

Add next 6 ingredients to same frying pan. Cook for about 12 minutes, stirring occasionally, until cabbage is softened. Add reserved orange juice mixture. Heat and stir for 1 minute until heated through.

Sprinkle with hazelnuts, green onion and bacon. Makes about 4 cups (1 L). Serve with Apple-Glazed Ham. Serves 12.

1 serving: 547 Calories; 32.5 g Total Fat (15.6 g Mono, 3.6 g Poly, 11.1 g Sat); 110 mg Cholesterol; 23 g Carbohydrate; 2 g Fibre; 39 g Protein; 2245 mg Sodium

Pictured on page 90.

Paré Pointer

Nothing is left—the stockings ran, the milk evaporated, the eggs scrambled and the fire went out!

Lamb Tagine

This rich and sweet lamb stew packs a pleasantly spicy heat and is made with the convenience of your slow cooker. It's perfect for the buffet table.

All-purpose flour	3 tbsp.	50 mL
Salt	1/2 tsp.	2 mL
Pepper	1/4 tsp.	1 mL
Boneless lamb shoulder, trimmed of fat and cut into 1 1/2 inch (3.8 cm) pieces	3 lbs.	1.4 kg
Cooking oil	2 tbsp.	30 mL
Cooking oil	2 tsp.	10 mL
Chopped onion	2 cups	500 mL
Brown sugar, packed	2 tsp.	10 mL
Garlic cloves, minced	2	2
Ground ginger	1 1/2 tsp.	7 mL
Ground cinnamon	1 tsp.	5 mL
Ground allspice	3/4 tsp.	4 mL
Dried crushed chilies	1/2 tsp.	2 mL
Prepared beef broth	2 cups	500 mL
Dried apricots, halved	1 cup	250 mL
Sun-dried tomatoes, softened in boiling water for 10 minutes before chopping	1/2 cup	125 mL

Combine first 3 ingredients in large resealable freezer bag. Add half of lamb. Seal bag. Toss until coated. Transfer lamb to plate. Repeat with remaining lamb. Discard any remaining flour mixture. Heat first amount of cooking oil in large frying pan on medium-high. Cook lamb, in 2 batches, for about 4 minutes, stirring occasionally, until browned. Transfer to 3 1/2 to 4 quart (3.5 to 4 L) slow cooker. Reduce heat to medium.

Heat second amount of cooking oil in same frying pan. Add onion. Cook for about 5 minutes, stirring often, until onion starts to soften.

Add next 6 ingredients. Heat and stir for about 2 minutes until garlic is fragrant. Add broth. Heat and stir, scraping any brown bits from bottom of pan, until boiling. Pour over lamb. Scatter apricots and tomatoes over top. Cook, covered, on Low for 8 to 10 hours or on High for 4 to 5 hours. Makes about 5 cups (1.25 L).

1 cup (250 mL): 772 Calories; 44.8 g Total Fat (19.6 g Mono, 5.4 g Poly, 16.3 g Sat); 196 mg Cholesterol; 36 g Carbohydrate; 4 g Fibre; 54 g Protein; 976 mg Sodium

Greek Lamb and Potatoes

This tender lamb roast is infused with the classic Greek seasonings. The accompaniment of lemony roasted potatoes would be wonderful with tzatziki.

Olive (or cooking) oil	1/3 cup	75 mL
Lemon juice	1/4 cup	60 mL
Chopped fresh oregano	1 tbsp.	15 mL
(or 3/4 tsp., 4 mL, dried)		
Chopped fresh rosemary	1 tbsp.	15 mL
(or 3/4 tsp., 4 mL, dried, crushed)		
Dijon mustard	1 tbsp.	15 mL
Coarsely ground pepper	1 tsp.	5 mL
Garlic cloves, minced	4	4
(or 1 tsp., 5 mL, powder)		
Grated lemon zest (see Tip, page 152)	1 tsp.	5 mL
Salt	1 tsp.	5 mL
Baby potatoes, larger ones halved	2 lbs.	900 g
Boneless leg of lamb	3 1/2 lbs.	1.6 kg
Olive (or cooking) oil	1 tbsp.	15 mL

Process first 9 ingredients in blender until smooth. Transfer 3 tbsp. (50 mL) to medium bowl.

Add potatoes. Toss.

Tie roast into uniform shape with butcher's string. Rub remaining olive oil mixture over roast.

Heat second amount of olive oil in large frying pan on medium-high. Add roast. Cook for about 5 minutes, turning occasionally, until browned on all sides. Place on greased wire rack set in medium roasting pan. Arrange potatoes around roast. Cook, uncovered, in 325°F (160°C) oven for about 1 hour 45 minutes until internal temperature reaches 160°F (71°C) for medium or until roast reaches desired doneness. Transfer to cutting board. Cover with foil. Let stand for 10 minutes. Cut into thin slices. Transfer potatoes with slotted spoon to serving bowl. Serves 8.

1 serving: 438 Calories; 20.0 g Total Fat (10.4 g Mono, 3.9 g Poly, 4.0 g Sat); 116 mg Cholesterol; 22 g Carbohydrate; 2 g Fibre; 40 g Protein; 410 mg Sodium

Ginger Chops With Mandarin Salsa

Moist chops are infused with gingery flavour and served with bright-tasting avocado and mandarin salsa for a punch of colour and freshness.

MANDARIN SALSA

Can of mandarin orange segments, drained, chopped	10 oz.	284 mL
Chopped avocado	1/2 cup	125 mL
Finely diced English cucumber (with peel)	1/4 cup	60 mL
Finely diced yellow pepper	1/4 cup	60 mL
Finely diced red onion	3 tbsp.	50 mL
Lime juice	3 tbsp.	50 mL
Cooking oil	1 tsp.	5 mL
Garlic clove, minced (or 1/4 tsp., 1 mL, powder)	1	1
Salt	1/8 tsp.	0.5 mL
Pepper	1/8 tsp.	0.5 mL
Ginger marmalade, larger pieces chopped	2 tbsp.	30 mL
Raspberry vinegar	2 tsp.	10 mL
Chili paste (sambal oelek)	1/2 tsp.	2 mL
Finely grated ginger root (or 1/8 tsp., 0.5 mL, ground ginger)	1/2 tsp.	2 mL
Ground cumin	1/4 tsp.	1 mL
Salt	1/4 tsp.	1 mL
Pepper, sprinkle		

CHOPS

Boneless centre-cut pork chops (about 3/4 inch, 2 cm, thick)	4	4
Chopped fresh cilantro (or parsley), optional	1 tbsp.	15 mL

(continued on next page)

Mandarin Salsa: Combine all 10 ingredients in small bowl. Makes about 2 cups (500 mL).

Chops: Put marmalade into medium microwave-safe bowl. Microwave, covered, on high for about 20 seconds until melted (see Tip, below). Add next 6 ingredients. Stir.

Arrange chops on greased wire rack set in foil-lined baking sheet with sides. Brush with marmalade mixture. Broil on centre rack in oven for 7 minutes. Turn. Brush with remaining marmalade mixture. Broil for about 7 minutes until internal temperature reaches 160°F (71°C). Transfer to large plate. Cover with foil. Let stand for 10 minutes. Spoon orange mixture over chops.

Sprinkle with cilantro. Serves 4.

1 serving: 307 Calories; 14.7 g Total Fat (7.3 g Mono, 1.5 g Poly, 4.4 g Sat); 67 mg Cholesterol; 19 g Carbohydrate; 2 g Fibre; 25 g Protein; 288 mg Sodium

Pictured on page 107.

 The microwaves used in our test kitchen are 900 watts—but microwaves are sold in many different powers. You should be able to find the wattage of yours by opening the door and looking for the mandatory label. If your microwave is more than 900 watts, you may need to reduce the cooking time. If it's less than 900 watts, you'll probably need to increase the cooking time.

Wild Rice-Stuffed Turkey

This year, break from tradition and stuff your Christmas turkey with a flavourful blend of wild rice, bacon, sweet apple and chili spice. Any leftover turkey can be used in Turkey Romaine Spears, page 14, or Turkey Wild Rice Soup, page 50.

Prepared chicken broth	3 cups	750 mL
Wild rice	1 1/2 cups	375 mL
Chopped fresh spinach leaves, lightly packed	3 cups	750 mL
Chopped dried apple	1/2 cup	125 mL
Chopped unsalted, roasted cashews	1/2 cup	125 mL
Chopped green onion	1/3 cup	75 mL
Bacon slices, cooked crisp and crumbled	3	3
Butter (or hard margarine), melted	2 tbsp.	30 mL
Pomegranate juice	2 tbsp.	30 mL
Salt	1/8 tsp.	0.5 mL
Pepper	1/2 tsp.	2 mL
Dried crushed chilies	1/4 tsp.	1 mL
Garlic clove, minced (or 1/4 tsp., 1 mL, powder)	1	1
Whole butter-basted turkey, giblets and neck removed	12 lbs.	5.4 kg
Cooking oil	2 tbsp.	30 mL
Salt	1/4 tsp.	1 mL
Pepper	1/4 tsp.	1 mL

Bring broth to a boil in medium saucepan. Add rice. Stir. Reduce heat to medium-low. Simmer, covered, for about 1 hour, without stirring, until rice is tender. Drain any remaining liquid. Transfer to large bowl.

Add next 11 ingredients. Stir.

Loosely fill body cavity of turkey with rice mixture. Secure with wooden picks or small metal skewers. Tie wings with butcher's string close to body. Tie legs to tail. Place on greased wire rack set in large roasting pan.

(continued on next page)

Rub cooking oil over surface of turkey. Sprinkle with salt and pepper. Cook, covered, in 325°F (160°C) oven for about 3 1/2 hours until meat thermometer inserted into thickest part of thigh reaches 180°F (82°C). Temperature of stuffing should reach at least 165°F (74°C). Transfer turkey to cutting board. Remove and discard butcher's string. Cover with foil. Let stand for 20 minutes. Internal temperature of turkey should rise to at least 185°F (85°C). Transfer stuffing to serving dish. Cover to keep warm. Makes about 5 cups (1.25 L) stuffing. Serve with turkey. Serves 12.

1 serving: 728 Calories; 33.3 g Total Fat (12.1 g Mono, 7.9 g Poly, 9.6 g Sat); 218 mg Cholesterol; 25 g Carbohydrate; 2 g Fibre; 79 g Protein; 547 mg Sodium

Pictured on page 108.

Paré Pointer

Mother grapefruit calling young grapefruit: "Come here, you little squirt."

Apricot Ginger Cornish Hens

These golden and aromatic Cornish hens make for an elegant main course,
offering delicate Asian flavours and sweet apricot—delicious and
broadly appealing.

Apricot jam	1/4 cup	60 mL
Chopped green onion	1/4 cup	60 mL
Apple cider vinegar	2 tbsp.	30 mL
Sesame oil (for flavour)	2 tbsp.	30 mL
Soy sauce	2 tbsp.	30 mL
Finely chopped ginger root	1 tbsp.	15 mL
(or 3/4 tsp., 4 mL, ground ginger)		
Dried crushed chilies	1/4 tsp.	1 mL
Garlic clove, minced	1	1
(or 1/4 tsp., 1 mL, powder)		
Cornish hens (1 1/2 – 2 lbs.,	2	2
680 g – 900 g, each)		
Butter (or hard margarine), melted	1 tbsp.	15 mL

Process first 8 ingredients in blender or food processor until almost smooth. Reserve 2 tbsp. (30 mL).

Place hens, backbone up, on cutting board. Cut down both sides of backbones with kitchen shears or sharp knife. Remove and discard backbones. Turn hens over. Press flat. Remove breastbones. Cut hens in half. Place in resealable freezer bag. Pour jam mixture over top. Seal bag. Marinate in refrigerator for 2 hours, turning occasionally. Remove hens. Discard remaining jam mixture.

Combine butter and reserved jam mixture in small cup. Stir. Place hens on greased wire rack set in foil-lined baking sheet with sides. Cook in 400°F (205°C) oven for about 35 minutes, brushing twice with butter mixture, until meat thermometer inserted in thickest part of thigh reaches 185°F (85°C). Transfer to large serving dish. Cover with foil. Let stand for 10 minutes. Serves 4.

1 serving: 283 Calories; 13.0 g Total Fat (2.3 g Mono, 1.3 g Poly, 3.8 g Sat); 141 mg Cholesterol; 11 g Carbohydrate; trace Fibre; 30 g Protein; 620 mg Sodium

1. Cranberry Confetti
   Slaw, page 52
2. Coconut-Crusted
   Chicken, page 94

Props: Le Gnome

1. Pepper Pork Stew,
   page 79
2. Ham With Sweet
   Cabbage, page 80

Sun-Dried Tomato Turkey Roll

Turkey breast is stuffed with sun-dried tomato, pecans and rice for a lovely main course, perfect for a more intimate holiday gathering.

Boneless, skinless turkey breast half	1 1/2 lbs.	680 g
Salt	1/8 tsp.	0.5 mL
Pepper	1/8 tsp.	0.5 mL
Cooked long-grain white rice	1/2 cup	125 mL
Finely chopped onion	1/4 cup	60 mL
Chopped pecans, toasted (see Tip, page 99)	3 tbsp.	50 mL
Sun-dried tomato pesto	3 tbsp.	50 mL
Garlic butter, melted	1 tbsp.	15 mL
Garlic butter, melted	1 tbsp.	15 mL
Sun-dried tomato pesto	1 tbsp.	15 mL

To butterfly turkey, cut horizontally lengthwise almost, but not quite through to other side. Open flat. Place between 2 sheets of plastic wrap. Pound with mallet or rolling pin to 1/4 inch (6 mm) thickness. Sprinkle with salt and pepper.

Combine next 5 ingredients in small bowl. Spread evenly over turkey. Roll up tightly, jelly-roll style, starting from long side. Tie with butcher's string. Place on greased wire rack set in baking sheet with sides.

Combine second amount of butter and pesto in small bowl. Brush 1 tbsp. (15 mL) over roll (see Safety Tip). Cook in 350°F (175°C) oven for 45 minutes. Brush with remaining pesto mixture. Cook for about 15 minutes until internal temperature of turkey reaches 170°F (77°C). Temperature of stuffing should reach at least 165°F (74°C). Transfer to cutting board. Remove and discard string. Cover with foil. Let stand for 10 minutes. Cut into 3/4 inch (2 cm) slices. Serves 6.

1 serving: 239 Calories; 10.6 g Total Fat (3.7 g Mono, 1.6 g Poly, 2.9 g Sat); 65 mg Cholesterol; 9 g Carbohydrate; 1 g Fibre; 27 g Protein; 169 mg Sodium

Safety Tip: Be sure to sanitize your brush after coating the raw turkey roll. A second amount of pesto mixture will be added once the turkey is cooked, so it is important that bacteria from the raw turkey do not contaminate the cooked meat.

Coq au Vin Blanc

This white wine version of a French favourite offers a more subtle flavour than the traditional red—but the taste experience is just as exquisite!

Bacon slices, cut into 1 inch (2.5 cm) pieces	6	6
Cooking oil	1 tsp.	5 mL
Bone-in chicken thighs (5 – 6 oz., 140 – 170 g, each)	8	8
Salt	1/2 tsp.	2 mL
Pepper	1/2 tsp.	2 mL
Halved fresh brown (or white) mushrooms	3 cups	750 mL
Garlic clove, minced (or 1/4 tsp., 1 mL, powder)	1	1
All-purpose flour	2 tbsp.	30 mL
Dry (or alcohol-free) white wine	2 cups	500 mL
Prepared chicken broth	1 cup	250 mL
Brandy	1/4 cup	60 mL
Tomato paste (see Tip, right)	2 tbsp.	30 mL
Pearl onions	5 oz.	140 g
Bay leaf	1	1
Dried thyme	1/2 tsp.	2 mL

Cook bacon in large frying pan on medium until crisp. Transfer with slotted spoon to paper towel-lined plate to drain. Reserve 2 tbsp. (30 mL) drippings in small cup. Discard remaining drippings.

Heat cooking oil in same frying pan. Sprinkle both sides of chicken with salt and pepper. Add to pan. Cook, partially covered, for about 5 minutes per side, until browned. Transfer to plate. Cover to keep warm.

Heat reserved drippings in same frying pan. Add mushrooms and garlic. Cook for about 5 minutes, stirring occasionally, until mushrooms are golden. Sprinkle with flour. Heat and stir for 1 minute.

(continued on next page)

Slowly add next 4 ingredients, stirring constantly until smooth. Heat and stir until boiling and thickened.

Add remaining 3 ingredients, bacon and chicken. Stir. Bring to a boil. Reduce heat to medium-low. Simmer, covered, for about 1 hour, stirring occasionally, until chicken is no longer pink inside and onions are tender. Remove and discard bay leaf. Serves 4.

1 serving: 533 Calories; 21.6 g Total Fat (8.6 g Mono, 4.2 g Poly, 6.7 g Sat); 129 mg Cholesterol; 14 g Carbohydrate; 2 g Fibre; 38 g Protein; 663 mg Sodium

Pictured on page 53.

 Try freezing tomato paste for 30 minutes before opening both ends and pushing the tube out. You'll be able to slice off what you need and wrap the rest for later.

Coconut-Crusted Chicken

These chicken breasts are stuffed with spinach and feta and can be served with or without an accompanying sauce of your choice. For added convenience, you can prepare this recipe in advance, leaving only the baking for your last-minute meal preparations.

Cooking oil	1/2 tsp.	2 mL
Finely chopped onion	1/2 cup	125 mL
Curry powder	1 tsp.	5 mL
Chopped fresh spinach leaves, lightly packed	2 cups	500 mL
Crumbled feta cheese	1/2 cup	125 mL
Boneless, skinless chicken breast halves (4 – 6 oz., 113 – 170 g, each)	6	6
Fine coconut	3/4 cup	175 mL
Finely chopped salted cashews	3/4 cup	175 mL
Chopped fresh parsley	1 tbsp.	15 mL
Large eggs	2	2
All-purpose flour	1/2 cup	125 mL
Curry powder	1 tbsp.	15 mL
Salt	1/2 tsp.	2 mL

Heat cooking oil in medium frying pan on medium. Add onion and curry powder. Cook for about 5 minutes, stirring often, until onion is softened.

Add spinach. Cook for about 2 minutes, stirring occasionally, until spinach is wilted and no liquid remains. Transfer to small bowl. Add cheese. Stir until cheese is melted. Chill for about 1 hour until cold.

Cut horizontal slit in thickest part of each chicken breast to create pocket. Fill with spinach mixture.

Combine next 3 ingredients in large shallow dish.

Beat eggs with fork in medium shallow bowl.

(continued on next page)

Combine remaining 3 ingredients on large plate. Coat chicken in flour mixture. Shake off any excess. Dip into egg. Press into coconut mixture until coated. Discard any remaining flour mixture, egg and coconut mixture. Arrange on greased foil-lined baking sheet with sides (see Note). Cook in 375°F (190°C) oven for about 25 minutes until internal temperature of chicken reaches 170°F (77°C). Temperature of stuffing should reach at least 165°F (74°C). Let stand for 5 minutes. Serves 6.

1 serving: *395 Calories; 22.3 g Total Fat (2.1 g Mono, 0.9 g Poly, 10.1 g Sat); 147 mg Cholesterol; 13 g Carbohydrate; 3 g Fibre; 35 g Protein; 473 mg Sodium*

Pictured on page 89.

Note: You can prepare the chicken to this point up to 4 hours in advance. Chill, covered, until ready to cook.

Paré Pointer

When the elephant hurt his foot, the zoo keeper called a toe truck.

Tuscan Winter Stew

Reminiscent of cassoulet, this savoury stew is hearty with chicken, beans, tomatoes and fresh herbs. Serve it with red wine and slices of focaccia.

Cooking oil	1 tbsp.	15 mL
Boneless, skinless chicken thighs, cut into 1 inch (2.5 cm) pieces	1 lb.	454 g
Salt	1/4 tsp.	1 mL
Pepper	1/4 tsp.	1 mL
Chopped onion	1 1/2 cups	375 mL
Garlic cloves, minced (or 1/2 tsp., 2 mL, powder)	2	2
Cans of mixed beans (19 oz., 540 mL, each), rinsed and drained	2	2
Prepared chicken broth	2 cups	500 mL
Chopped sun-dried tomatoes in oil, blotted dry	1/2 cup	125 mL
Chopped fresh rosemary (or 1/2 tsp., 2 mL, dried, crushed)	2 tsp.	10 mL
Chopped fresh thyme (or 1/2 tsp., 2 mL, dried)	2 tsp.	10 mL
Chopped fresh parsley	2 tsp.	10 mL

Heat cooking oil in large saucepan or Dutch oven on medium-high. Add chicken. Sprinkle with salt and pepper. Cook for about 5 minutes, stirring occasionally, until starting to brown.

Add onion and garlic. Cook for about 5 minutes, stirring often, until onion is softened.

Add next 3 ingredients. Stir. Bring to a boil. Reduce heat to medium. Boil gently, partially covered, for about 10 minutes until chicken is no longer pink inside.

Add rosemary and thyme. Heat and stir for about 3 minutes until herbs are fragrant.

Sprinkle with parsley. Makes about 6 cups (1.5 L).

1 cup (250 mL): 371 Calories; 11.5 g Total Fat (4.8 g Mono, 2.9 g Poly, 2.3 g Sat); 50 mg Cholesterol; 40 g Carbohydrate; 10 g Fibre; 27 g Protein; 796 mg Sodium

Curry Vegetable Pilaf

A golden casserole of rice and chickpeas, with warm curry flavours and a fresh cilantro sprinkle. This hearty vegetarian recipe could also serve as a side dish.

Cooking oil	1 tbsp.	15 mL
Chopped onion	2 cups	500 mL
Finely chopped fennel bulb (white part only)	1 cup	250 mL
Mild curry paste	2 tbsp.	30 mL
Finely grated ginger root (or 1/2 tsp., 2 mL, ground ginger)	2 tsp.	10 mL
Granulated sugar	1 tsp.	5 mL
Garlic cloves, minced (or 1/2 tsp., 2 mL, powder)	2	2
Salt	1/2 tsp.	2 mL
Pepper	1/4 tsp.	1 mL
Can of chickpeas (garbanzo beans), rinsed and drained	19 oz.	540 mL
Diced zucchini (with peel)	2 cups	500 mL
White basmati rice	1 1/2 cups	375 mL
Diced red pepper	1 cup	250 mL
Hot prepared vegetable broth	3 cups	750 mL
Chopped fresh cilantro (or parsley)	3 tbsp.	50 mL

Heat cooking oil in large frying pan on medium. Add onion and fennel. Cook for about 10 minutes, stirring often, until onion starts to soften.

Add next 6 ingredients. Cook for about 3 minutes, stirring occasionally, until garlic is fragrant.

Add next 4 ingredients. Stir. Spread evenly in greased 9 x 13 inch (23 x 33 cm) baking dish.

Add broth. Cover tightly with foil. Cook in 400°F (205°C) oven for about 35 minutes until rice is tender. Let stand, covered, for about 10 minutes until liquid is absorbed.

Sprinkle with cilantro. Makes about 12 cups (3 L).

1 cup (250 mL): 171 Calories; 2.4 g Total Fat (1.0 g Mono, 0.9 g Poly, 0.2 g Sat); 0 mg Cholesterol; 33 g Carbohydrate; 3 g Fibre; 5 g Protein; 348 mg Sodium

Pictured on page 54.

Mushroom Risotto Parcels

Attractive phyllo bundles hold a cheesy mushroom mixture packed with flavour. These can be made in advance and frozen in an airtight container for up to three months.

Prepared vegetable broth	1 cup	250 mL
Arborio rice	1/2 cup	125 mL
Olive (or cooking) oil	1 tbsp.	15 mL
Sliced fresh brown (or white) mushrooms	4 cups	1 L
Sliced leek (white part only)	1 1/2 cups	375 mL
Garlic clove, minced	1	1
(or 1/4 tsp., 1 mL, powder)		
Dry (or alcohol-free) white wine	1/4 cup	60 mL
Chopped fresh spinach leaves, lightly packed	2 cups	500 mL
Sun-dried tomato pesto	2 tbsp.	30 mL
Grated Italian cheese blend	1 1/2 cups	375 mL
Chopped pine nuts, toasted (see Tip, right)	2 tbsp.	30 mL
Coarsely ground pepper	1/4 tsp.	1 mL
Phyllo pastry sheets, thawed according to package directions	6	6
Butter (or hard margarine), melted	1/2 cup	125 mL
Grated Parmesan cheese	6 tbsp.	100 mL

Bring broth to a boil in small saucepan. Add rice. Reduce heat to medium-low. Simmer, covered, for 15 minutes, without stirring. Remove from heat. Let stand, covered, for about 5 minutes until rice is tender and liquid is absorbed. Fluff with fork.

Heat olive oil in large frying pan on medium. Add next 3 ingredients. Cook for about 15 minutes, stirring often, until leek is softened and liquid is evaporated.

Add wine. Heat and stir for about 2 minutes until liquid is evaporated.

Add spinach and pesto. Stir. Cook for about 2 minutes, stirring occasionally, until spinach is wilted. Remove from heat. Let stand for about 20 minutes until cool.

(continued on next page)

Add next 3 ingredients and rice. Stir.

Place 1 pastry sheet on work surface. Cover remaining sheets with damp towel to prevent drying. Brush sheet with butter. Sprinkle with 1 tbsp. (15 mL) Parmesan cheese. Fold in half crosswise. Spoon about 2/3 cup (150 mL) rice mixture onto bottom short edge. Fold in sides to cover filling. Roll up from bottom to enclose. Arrange, seam-side down, on greased baking sheet with sides. Brush with butter. Repeat with remaining pastry sheets, butter and rice mixture (see Note). Bake in 375°F (190°C) oven for about 25 minutes until golden. Makes 6 parcels.

1 parcel: 377 Calories; 24.2 g Total Fat (6.4 g Mono, 2.4 g Poly, 12.2 g Sat); 50 mg Cholesterol; 24 g Carbohydrate; 2 g Fibre; 16 g Protein; 675 mg Sodium

Pictured on page 54.

Note: Parcels can be frozen before baking. Freeze directly on baking sheet, then transfer to airtight container. Bake from frozen in 375°F (190°C) oven for about 40 minutes until golden and heated through.

 When toasting nuts, seeds or coconut, cooking times will vary for each type of nut—so never toast them together. For small amounts, place ingredient in an ungreased shallow frying pan. Heat on medium for 3 to 5 minutes, stirring often, until golden. For larger amounts, spread ingredient evenly in an ungreased shallow pan. Bake in a 350°F (175°C) oven for 5 to 10 minutes, stirring or shaking often, until golden.

Vegetable Pesto Lasagna

This hearty lasagna is so full of cheese, fresh vegetables and pesto that you won't even miss the meat! A hint of nutmeg adds a unique flavour accent.

Cooking oil	1 tbsp.	15 mL
Chopped onion	2 cups	500 mL
Chopped red pepper	2 cups	500 mL
Chopped zucchini (with peel)	2 cups	500 mL
Sliced fresh white mushrooms	1 cup	250 mL
Garlic cloves, minced	3	3
(or 3/4 tsp., 4 mL, powder)		
Pepper	1/4 tsp.	1 mL
Can of diced tomatoes (with juice)	14 oz.	398 mL
Butter (or hard margarine)	2 tbsp.	30 mL
All-purpose flour	3 tbsp.	50 mL
Milk	3 cups	750 mL
Grated Parmesan cheese	1/2 cup	125 mL
Ground nutmeg	1/4 tsp.	1 mL
Pepper, sprinkle		
Ricotta cheese	2 cups	500 mL
Basil pesto	1/3 cup	75 mL
Oven-ready lasagna noodles	9	9
Grated mozzarella cheese	1 cup	250 mL

Heat cooking oil in large frying pan on medium-high. Add next 6 ingredients. Cook for about 10 minutes, stirring often, until onion is softened and liquid is evaporated.

Add tomatoes. Stir. Remove from heat.

Melt butter in medium saucepan on medium. Add flour. Heat and stir for 1 minute. Slowly add milk, stirring constantly until smooth. Heat and stir until boiling and thickened.

(continued on next page)

Add next 3 ingredients. Stir. Remove from heat.

Combine ricotta cheese and pesto in small bowl.

Layer ingredients in greased 9 x 13 inch (23 x 33 cm) baking dish as follows:

1. 3 noodles
2. Half of pesto mixture
3. Half of tomato mixture
4. 3 noodles
5. Remaining pesto mixture
6. Remaining tomato mixture
7. Remaining noodles
8. Parmesan cheese mixture

Sprinkle with mozzarella cheese. Cover with greased foil. Bake in 350°F (175°C) oven for 45 minutes. Remove foil. Bake for about 50 minutes until top is golden. Let stand for 15 minutes. Cuts into 8 pieces.

1 piece: 414 Calories; 20.6 g Total Fat (1.9 g Mono, 0.9 g Poly, 9.4 g Sat); 49 mg Cholesterol; 33 g Carbohydrate; 3 g Fibre; 24 g Protein; 631 mg Sodium

Paré Pointer
To eat spaghetti properly, use your noodle.

Feta and Tomato Pasta

An appetizing casserole with the crowd-pleasing flavours of tasty tomatoes and feta—best served with fresh French bread!

Water	12 cups	3 L
Salt	1 1/2 tsp.	7 mL
Fusilli pasta	3 cups	750 mL
Cooking oil	2 tsp.	10 mL
Sliced fresh white mushrooms	2 cups	500 mL
Chopped onion	1 cup	250 mL
Chopped red pepper	2 cups	500 mL
Chopped sun-dried tomatoes in oil, blotted dry	3/4 cup	175 mL
Dried oregano	2 tsp.	10 mL
Garlic cloves, minced (or 1/2 tsp., 2 mL, powder)	2	2
Pepper	1/2 tsp.	2 mL
Can of tomato sauce	25 oz.	680 mL
Can of diced tomatoes, drained	14 oz.	398 mL
Granulated sugar	2 tsp.	10 mL
Crumbled feta cheese	1 cup	250 mL
Grated Parmesan cheese	1/2 cup	125 mL

Combine water and salt in Dutch oven. Bring to a boil. Add pasta. Boil, uncovered, for 7 to 9 minutes, stirring occasionally, until tender but firm. Drain. Return to same pot. Cover to keep warm.

Heat cooking oil in large frying pan on medium. Add mushrooms and onion. Cook for about 8 minutes, stirring often, until onion is softened.

Add next 5 ingredients. Cook for about 4 minutes, stirring occasionally, until red pepper is tender-crisp.

Add next 3 ingredients. Stir. Bring to a boil. Simmer, uncovered, for 10 minutes. Add to pasta.

Add feta cheese. Stir. Transfer to serving bowl.

Sprinkle with Parmesan cheese. Makes about 9 cups (2.25 L).

1 cup (250 mL): 264 Calories; 8.5 g Total Fat (2.2 g Mono, 0.8 g Poly, 3.7 g Sat); 19 mg Cholesterol; 37 g Carbohydrate; 4 g Fibre; 11 g Protein; 840 mg Sodium

Spiced Veggies and Rice

Apples and spice make everything nice in this exotic blend of brown rice and veggies.

Water	1 1/3 cups	325 mL
Salt, sprinkle		
Long-grain brown rice	2/3 cup	150 mL
Cooking oil	2 tsp.	10 mL
Sliced leek (white part only)	1 cup	250 mL
Chopped onion	3/4 cup	175 mL
Thinly sliced carrot	3/4 cup	175 mL
Chopped unpeeled tart apple (such as Granny Smith)	1/2 cup	125 mL
Ground coriander	1 tsp.	5 mL
Ground cumin	1 tsp.	5 mL
Cayenne pepper	1/8 tsp.	0.5 mL
Prepared chicken broth	1/4 cup	60 mL

Combine water and salt in small saucepan. Bring to a boil. Add rice. Stir. Reduce heat to medium-low. Simmer, covered, for about 35 minutes, without stirring, until rice is tender. Remove from heat. Let stand, covered, for about 5 minutes until liquid is absorbed.

Heat cooking oil in medium saucepan on medium. Add next 4 ingredients. Cook for about 5 minutes, stirring often, until onion is softened.

Add next 3 ingredients. Stir.

Add broth. Stir. Bring to a boil. Boil gently, covered, for about 4 minutes, stirring occasionally, until liquid is evaporated and carrot is tender. Add rice. Stir until heated through. Makes about 2 3/4 cups (675 mL).

1 cup (250 mL): 179 Calories; 3.5 g Total Fat (1.7 g Mono, 1.1 g Poly, 0.4 g Sat); 0 mg Cholesterol; 34 g Carbohydrate; 4 g Fibre; 4 g Protein; 122 mg Sodium

Apple Cabbage Braise

This vibrant blend of tender cabbage and soft apple pieces has a surprisingly delicate flavour. It makes a big batch, so you can portion and freeze it in airtight containers for up to one month.

Cooking oil	2 tbsp.	30 mL
Shredded red cabbage, lightly packed	8 cups	2 L
Sliced onion	1 cup	250 mL
Apple cider vinegar	1/2 cup	125 mL
Apple juice	1/2 cup	125 mL
Prepared chicken broth	1/2 cup	125 mL
Cumin seed	2 tsp.	10 mL
Bay leaf	1	1
Chopped peeled tart apple (such as Granny Smith)	2 cups	500 mL
Granulated sugar	2 tbsp.	30 mL
Salt	1/4 tsp.	1 mL
Pepper	1/4 tsp.	1 mL

Heat cooking oil in Dutch oven on medium. Add cabbage and onion. Cook for about 5 minutes, stirring often, until starting to soften.

Add next 5 ingredients. Stir. Bring to a boil. Reduce heat to medium-low. Cook, covered, for 30 minutes, stirring occasionally.

Add remaining 4 ingredients. Stir. Cook, covered, for about 15 minutes, stirring once, until cabbage is tender. Remove and discard bay leaf. Makes about 6 cups (1.5 L).

1 cup (250 mL): 130 Calories; 5.1 g Total Fat (2.9 g Mono, 1.5 g Poly, 0.4 g Sat); 0 mg Cholesterol; 22 g Carbohydrate; 4 g Fibre; 3 g Protein; 200 mg Sodium

Paré Pointer

The favourite holiday destination for chickens is San Di-egg-o.

Sides & Condiments

Maple Mustard Green Beans

A classic green bean side—this version has pretty Dijon mustard seeds, red pepper pieces and a hint of maple sweetness.

Cooking oil	2 tsp.	10 mL
Finely chopped onion	2 tbsp.	30 mL
Finely chopped red pepper	2 tbsp.	30 mL
Balsamic vinegar	3 tbsp.	50 mL
Dijon mustard (with whole seeds)	2 tbsp.	30 mL
Maple syrup	1 tbsp.	15 mL
Salt	1/4 tsp.	1 mL
Pepper	1/8 tsp.	0.5 mL
Fresh (or frozen) whole green beans, halved crosswise	7 cups	1.75 L
Salt	1/4 tsp.	1 mL

Heat cooking oil in small frying pan on medium. Add onion and red pepper. Cook for about 2 minutes, stirring often, until softened. Remove from heat.

Add next 5 ingredients. Stir.

Pour water into large saucepan until about 1 inch (2.5 cm) deep. Add green beans and salt. Cover. Bring to a boil. Reduce heat to medium. Boil gently for about 5 minutes until bright green and tender-crisp (see Note). Drain. Add onion mixture. Toss until coated. Makes about 6 1/2 cups (1.6 L).

1 cup (250 mL): 61 Calories; 1.8 g Total Fat (0.8 g Mono, 0.4 g Poly, 0.1 g Sat); 0 mg Cholesterol; 10 g Carbohydrate; 2 g Fibre; 1 g Protein; 284 mg Sodium

Pictured on page 107.

Note: If using frozen green beans, reduce cooking time to about 1 minute.

Potato Parsnip Latkes

Tender-crisp potato cakes with flavourful parsnip and onion—an appealing side traditionally served during Hanukkah. Serve with sour cream or applesauce for dipping.

Grated peeled potato	1 1/2 cups	375 mL
Grated parsnip	1 cup	250 mL
Finely chopped onion	1/2 cup	125 mL
Large egg, fork-beaten	1	1
All-purpose flour	1/3 cup	75 mL
Lemon juice	2 tsp.	10 mL
Italian seasoning	1/2 tsp.	2 mL
Salt	1/4 tsp.	1 mL
Pepper	1/4 tsp.	1 mL
Cooking oil	1/4 cup	60 mL

Combine first 3 ingredients in fine sieve. Let stand over medium bowl for 15 minutes. Squeeze vegetables to remove excess moisture.

Combine next 6 ingredients in large bowl. Add potato mixture. Stir well.

Heat 2 tbsp. (30 mL) cooking oil in large frying pan on medium. Drop 6 portions of potato mixture into pan, using 3 tbsp. (50 mL) for each. Press down lightly to 3 inch (7.5 cm) diameter. Cook for about 4 minutes per side until golden brown. Transfer to paper towel-lined plate to drain. Cover to keep warm. Repeat with remaining cooking oil and potato mixture. Makes about 12 latkes.

1 latke: 70 Calories; 4.0 g Total Fat (2.2 g Mono, 1.1 g Poly, 0.4 g Sat); 18 mg Cholesterol; 8 g Carbohydrate; 1 g Fibre; 1 g Protein; 88 mg Sodium

1. Maple Mustard Green Beans, page 105
2. Light Rye Rolls, page 28
3. Ginger Chops With Mandarin Salsa, page 84

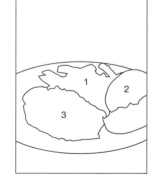

Pepper Cran-Cherry Sauce

A lovely and complex sweet-tart sauce with a hint of orange flavour and a peppery bite—this pairs beautifully with your holiday meal of turkey or pork roast.

Granulated sugar	3/4 cup	175 mL
Orange juice	1/2 cup	125 mL
Water	1/2 cup	125 mL
Bag of fresh (or frozen) cranberries	12 oz.	340 g
Chopped dried cherries	1/2 cup	125 mL
Coarsely ground pepper	1 tsp.	5 mL
Grated orange zest (see Tip, page 152)	1/2 tsp.	2 mL

Stir first 3 ingredients in medium saucepan until sugar is dissolved. Bring to a boil.

Add remaining 4 ingredients. Stir. Bring to a boil. Reduce heat to medium. Boil gently, uncovered, for about 10 minutes, stirring occasionally, until slightly thickened. Makes about 2 1/3 cups (575 mL).

1 tbsp. (15 mL): 22 Calories; trace Total Fat (0 g Mono, 0 g Poly, 0 g Sat); 0 mg Cholesterol; 6 g Carbohydrate; 1 g Fibre; trace Protein; trace Sodium

Pictured at left.

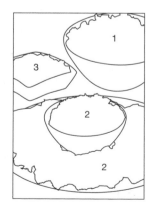

1. Roasted Broccoli and Brussels, page 116
2. Wild Rice-Stuffed Turkey, page 86
3. Pepper Cran-Cherry Sauce, above

Props: Le Gnome

Fennel Potato Gratin

Fennel imparts a delightfully mild licorice flavour to this creamy gratin.

Cooking oil	1 tsp.	5 mL
Thinly sliced fennel bulb (white part only)	4 cups	1 L
Garlic cloves, minced	2	2
(or 1/2 tsp., 2 mL, powder)		
Dried thyme	1/4 tsp.	1 mL
Salt	1/4 tsp.	1 mL
Pepper	1/8 tsp.	0.5 mL
All-purpose flour	2 tbsp.	30 mL
Dried rosemary, crushed	1/2 tsp.	2 mL
Salt	1/4 tsp.	1 mL
Pepper	1/8 tsp.	0.5 mL
Thinly sliced peeled baking potato (see Note)	4 cups	1 L
Half-and-half cream	1 cup	250 mL
Prepared vegetable broth	1/2 cup	125 mL
Grated Parmesan cheese	2/3 cup	150 mL
Chopped fresh parsley (optional)	1 tbsp.	15 mL

Heat cooking oil in large frying pan on medium. Add next 5 ingredients. Cook, covered, for about 10 minutes, stirring occasionally, until fennel is softened.

Combine next 4 ingredients in small cup.

To assemble, layer ingredients in greased 2 quart (2 L) casserole as follows:

1. 1/3 of potato slices
2. 1/2 of flour mixture
3. 1/2 of fennel mixture
4. 1/3 of potato slices
5. Remaining flour mixture
6. Remaining fennel mixture
7. Remaining potato slices

Combine cream and broth in small bowl. Pour over potato slices. Cover with greased foil. Bake in 350°F (175°C) oven for 1 hour. Carefully remove foil.

(continued on next page)

Sides & Condiments

Sprinkle cheese over top. Bake in oven for about 15 minutes until potato is tender and cheese is melted and browned.

Sprinkle with parsley. Makes about 8 cups (2 L).

1 cup (250 mL): 251 Calories; 7.4 g Total Fat (1.4 g Mono, 0.4 g Poly, 3.7 g Sat); 18 mg Cholesterol; 40 g Carbohydrate; 8 g Fibre; 9 g Protein; 456 mg Sodium

Pictured on page 36.

Note: Evenly sliced vegetables are one of the secrets to a good scallop. Use a mandolin slicer or food processor to ensure equal thickness.

Red and Green Couscous

This nutritious couscous blend is reminiscent of Italian cuisine, with tomato, fresh herbs and garlic—an attractive and versatile side dish.

Olive (or cooking) oil	1 tbsp.	15 mL
Chopped onion	1 cup	250 mL
Garlic cloves, minced	2	2
(or 1/2 tsp., 2 mL, powder)		
Prepared chicken broth	2 cups	500 mL
Balsamic vinegar	2 tbsp.	30 mL
Whole-wheat couscous	1 1/4 cups	300 mL
Finely diced seeded tomato	1 1/2 cups	375 mL
Chopped fresh basil	2 tbsp.	30 mL
Chopped fresh parsley	2 tbsp.	30 mL

Heat olive oil in large saucepan on medium-high. Add onion. Cook for about 5 minutes, stirring often, until softened. Add garlic. Heat and stir for 1 minute.

Add broth and vinegar. Bring to a boil.

Add couscous. Stir. Remove from heat. Let stand, covered, for about 5 minutes until liquid is absorbed. Fluff with fork.

Add remaining 3 ingredients. Stir. Makes about 6 cups (1.5 L).

1 cup (250 mL): 146 Calories; 3.4 g Total Fat (1.6 g Mono, 0.9 g Poly, 0.3 g Sat); 0 mg Cholesterol; 25 g Carbohydrate; 4 g Fibre; 6 g Protein; 264 mg Sodium

Creamy Roasted Garlic Potatoes

A delicious mashed potato casserole designed to be made ahead—one less thing to worry about before a big dinner. This can be made in the morning and reheated later, or prepared and frozen up to a month in advance.

Garlic bulbs	2	2
Cooking oil	1 tbsp.	15 mL
Peeled potatoes, cut up	3 lbs.	1.4 kg
Half-and-half cream	2/3 cup	150 mL
Butter (or hard margarine)	3 tbsp.	50 mL
Finely chopped green onion	3 tbsp.	50 mL
Salt	1 tsp.	5 mL
Pepper	1/4 tsp.	1 mL
Grated havarti cheese	1 cup	250 mL

Coarsely ground pepper, for garnish

Trim 1/4 inch (6 mm) from garlic bulbs to expose tops of cloves, leaving bulbs intact. Drizzle with cooking oil. Wrap loosely in greased foil. Cook in 375°F (190°C) oven for about 45 minutes until tender. Let stand until cool enough to handle. Squeeze garlic bulbs to remove cloves from skin. Discard skin. Mash garlic with fork on small plate until smooth.

Pour water into large saucepan until 1 inch (2.5 cm) deep. Add potato. Cover. Bring to a boil. Reduce heat to medium. Boil gently for 12 to 15 minutes until tender. Drain. Mash.

Add next 5 ingredients and garlic. Mash.

Add cheese. Stir well. Spread evenly in well-greased 2 quart (2 L) casserole.

Sprinkle with pepper. Makes about 8 1/2 cups (2.1 L).

1 cup (250 mL): 275 Calories; 12.8 g Total Fat (2.6 g Mono, 0.8 g Poly, 7.4 g Sat); 29 mg Cholesterol; 34 g Carbohydrate; 3 g Fibre; 6 g Protein; 764 mg Sodium

Pictured on page 53.

Make Ahead: Stores in airtight container in refrigerator for up to 2 days or in freezer for up to 1 month. Thaw in refrigerator before cooking. Cook, covered, in 350°F (175°C) oven for about 1 1/2 hours until internal temperature reaches 165°F (74°C).

Slow Cooker Stuffing

A rustic stuffing that makes a big batch for the family to dig into, perfectly textured with sweet bits of squash and red pepper. Best of all, it saves valuable space in the oven—but keep in mind that this recipe cannot be easily doubled.

Butter (or hard margarine)	2 tbsp.	30 mL
Cooking oil	2 tbsp.	30 mL
Diced butternut squash	2 cups	500 mL
Chopped onion	1 1/2 cups	375 mL
Sliced celery	1 1/2 cups	375 mL
Diced red pepper	1 cup	250 mL
Dried marjoram	1/2 tsp.	2 mL
Dried sage	1/2 tsp.	2 mL
Dried thyme	1/2 tsp.	2 mL
Poultry seasoning	1/2 tsp.	2 mL
Pepper	1/4 tsp.	1 mL
Unseasoned croutons (see Tip, below)	6 cups	1.5 L
Box of chicken stovetop stuffing mix	4 1/4 oz.	120 g
Prepared chicken broth	1 3/4 cups	425 mL

Heat butter and cooking oil in large frying pan on medium until butter is melted. Add next 9 ingredients. Cook for about 10 minutes, stirring often, until squash is tender-crisp. Remove from heat.

Combine croutons and stuffing mix in large bowl. Drizzle with broth. Toss until coated. Add squash mixture. Toss. Transfer to well-greased 4 to 5 quart (4 to 5 L) slow cooker. Cook, covered, on Low for about 3 hours or on High for about 1 1/2 hours until internal temperature reaches 165°F (74°C). Makes about 10 cups (2.5 L).

1 cup (250 mL): 215 Calories; 8.0 g Total Fat (2.9 g Mono, 1.3 g Poly, 2.0 g Sat); 6 mg Cholesterol; 31 g Carbohydrate; 3 g Fibre; 5 g Protein; 493 mg Sodium

 tip You can use coarse dry bread crumbs that look like croutons, or make your own by cutting bread in small cubes and drying in a low oven.

Mango Cranberry Chutney

Mango chutney with a punch of heat and sweet bites of cranberry. Change up the traditional cranberry sauce and serve this with your roast turkey or pork! If you happen to have any leftover, it makes an exceptional sandwich spread.

Cooking oil	1 tbsp.	15 mL
Chopped onion	1 cup	250 mL
Curry powder	1 tbsp.	15 mL
Finely grated ginger root	1 tbsp.	15 mL
(or 3/4 tsp., 4 mL, ground ginger)		
Garlic clove, minced	1	1
(or 1/4 tsp., 1 mL, powder)		
Dried crushed chilies	1/8 tsp.	0.5 mL
Chopped frozen mango pieces	3 cups	750 mL
Pineapple juice	1/2 cup	125 mL
Apple cider vinegar	1/3 cup	75 mL
Brown sugar, packed	1/4 cup	60 mL
Chopped dried cranberries	1/4 cup	60 mL
Salt, sprinkle		
Pepper, sprinkle		

Heat cooking oil in large saucepan on medium. Add next 5 ingredients. Cook for about 5 minutes, stirring often, until onion starts to soften.

Add next 4 ingredients. Bring to a boil. Reduce heat to medium-low. Simmer, uncovered, for about 20 minutes, stirring occasionally, until mixture is thickened. Remove from heat.

Add remaining 3 ingredients. Stir well. Makes about 3 cups (750 mL).

1 tbsp. (15 mL): 18 Calories; 0.3 g Total Fat (0.2 g Mono, 0.1 g Poly, trace Sat); 0 mg Cholesterol; 4 g Carbohydrate; trace Fibre; trace Protein; 1 mg Sodium

Herbed Parsnips

Rustic, herb-speckled parsnips with rich, buttery flavour. The fresh herbs elevate this to company fare.

Diagonally sliced parsnip (about 1/2 inch, 12 mm, slices), see Note	4 cups	1 L
Butter (or hard margarine)	2 tbsp.	30 mL
Granulated sugar	1 tsp.	5 mL
Chopped fresh parsley (or 1/2 tsp., 2 mL, flakes)	1 tbsp.	15 mL
Chopped fresh rosemary (or 1/4 tsp., 1 mL, dried, crushed)	1 tsp.	5 mL
Chopped fresh thyme (or 1/4 tsp., 1 mL, dried)	1 tsp.	5 mL
Salt	1/8 tsp.	0.5 mL
Coarsely ground pepper	1/4 tsp.	1 mL

Pour water into medium saucepan until about 1 inch (2.5 cm) deep. Add parsnip. Bring to a boil. Reduce heat to medium. Boil gently, covered, for about 12 minutes until tender. Drain. Return to same pot.

Add butter and sugar. Stir. Reduce heat to medium-low. Cook, uncovered, for about 2 minutes, stirring occasionally, until parsnips are coated.

Add remaining 5 ingredients. Stir. Makes about 3 cups (750 mL).

1 cup (250 mL): 205 Calories; 8.1 g Total Fat (2.2 g Mono, 0.4 g Poly, 4.9 g Sat); 20 mg Cholesterol; 33 g Carbohydrate; 9 g Fibre; 2 g Protein; 169 mg Sodium

Note: To ensure parsnips achieve an even doneness, halve thick ends lengthwise before slicing for evenly sized pieces.

Paré Pointer

The teacher has a frog in his throat. He could croak any minute now.

Roasted Broccoli and Brussels

Get your greens this season with these appetizing roasted veggies, dressed up with lemon, mild chili and a sprinkle of sesame seeds.

Cooking oil	1 tbsp.	15 mL
Lemon juice	1 tbsp.	15 mL
Chili paste (sambal oelek)	1/2 tsp.	2 mL
Salt	1/4 tsp.	1 mL
Pepper	1/2 tsp.	2 mL
Ground coriander	1/4 tsp.	1 mL
Broccoli florets, halved	4 cups	1 L
Brussels sprouts (about 1 lb., 454 g), trimmed and halved lengthwise (see Note)	4 cups	1 L
Pearl onions, larger ones halved	1 cup	250 mL
Garlic cloves, thinly sliced	3	3
Sesame seeds, toasted (see Tip, page 99)	1 tbsp.	15 mL
Grated lemon zest (see Tip, page 152)	1/2 tsp.	2 mL
Sesame oil (for flavour)	1/2 tsp.	2 mL

Combine first 6 ingredients in large bowl.

Add next 4 ingredients. Toss. Arrange in single layer on greased large baking sheet with sides. Cook in 400°F (205°C) oven for about 23 minutes, stirring at halftime, until Brussels sprouts and broccoli are browned and tender-crisp. Return to large bowl.

Add remaining 3 ingredients. Toss. Makes about 6 cups (1.5 L).

1 cup (250 mL): 103 Calories; 3.8 g Total Fat (1.4 g Mono, 0.9 g Poly, 0.3 g Sat); 0 mg Cholesterol; 15 g Carbohydrate; 4 g Fibre; 5 g Protein; 144 mg Sodium

Pictured on page 108.

Note: Select Brussels sprouts that are heavy for their size and bright green with tight leaves. Small heads, about 1 inch (2.5 cm) in diameter, are best. Before cooking, remove any brown leaves and trim the stem ends.

White Chocolate Panforte

A candy thermometer is an invaluable tool to ensure the success of this recipe. Panforte (pronounced pan-FOHR-teh) is a traditional Italian sweet and will store in an airtight container in a cool, dry place for up to one month.

Dried cranberries	1 cup	250 mL
Salted cashews	1 cup	250 mL
Whole natural almonds	1 cup	250 mL
All-purpose flour	3/4 cup	175 mL
Ground cinnamon	1/2 tsp.	2 mL
Granulated sugar	1 cup	250 mL
Liquid honey	3/4 cup	175 mL
White chocolate baking squares (1 oz., 28 g, each), chopped	4	4

Combine first 5 ingredients in large bowl.

Stir sugar and honey in small saucepan on medium until sugar is dissolved. Bring to a boil. Boil for about 1 1/2 minutes without stirring, brushing sides of pan with wet pastry brush to dissolve any sugar crystals, until mixture reaches soft ball stage (234°F to 240°F, 112°C to 116°C) on candy thermometer or until small amount dropped into very cold water forms a soft ball that flattens on its own accord when removed (see Note). Remove from heat. Add to nut mixture. Stir well.

Add chocolate. Stir until melted. Line greased 8 x 8 inch (20 x 20 cm) pan with parchment paper, leaving a 1 inch (2.5 cm) overhang on 2 sides. Spread chocolate mixture evenly in pan. Bake in 325°F (160°C) oven for about 20 minutes until edges are golden. Let stand in pan on wire rack until completely cooled. Invert onto cutting board. Cut in half. Cut each half crosswise into 1/2 inch (12 mm) bars. Makes about 28 bars.

1 bar: 157 Calories; 6.9 g Total Fat (1.6 g Mono, 0.6 g Poly, 1.6 g Sat); 1 mg Cholesterol; 23 g Carbohydrate; 1 g Fibre; 3 g Protein; 41 mg Sodium

Pictured on page 126.

Note: Test your candy thermometer before each use. Bring water to a boil. Candy thermometer should read 212°F (100°C) at sea level. Adjust recipe temperature up or down based on test results. For example, if your thermometer reads 206°F (97°C), subtract 6°F (3°C) from each temperature called for in recipe.

White Chocolate Cherry Cookies

Pretty and appealing Christmas cookies with decadent white chocolate and macadamias. Slice and bake one roll to give away, and keep the other for your family! The dough must be chilled overnight, so you could easily bake up a batch of fresh cookies during a casual get-together.

Butter (or hard margarine), softened	1 cup	250 mL
Brown sugar, packed	3/4 cup	175 mL
Granulated sugar	1/2 cup	125 mL
Large egg	1	1
Almond extract	1 tsp.	5 mL
All-purpose flour	2 1/2 cups	625 mL
Baking powder	1/2 tsp.	2 mL
Baking soda	1/2 tsp.	2 mL
Salt	1/4 tsp.	1 mL
Raw macadamia nuts, chopped	1 cup	250 mL
Red glazed cherries, chopped	1 cup	250 mL
White chocolate baking squares (1 oz., 28 g, each), chopped	4	4

Beat first 3 ingredients in large bowl until light and fluffy. Add egg and extract. Beat well.

Combine next 4 ingredients in small bowl. Add to butter mixture. Stir until no dry flour remains.

Add remaining 3 ingredients. Mix well. Divide into 2 portions. Roll into 9 inch (23 cm) long logs. Wrap with plastic wrap. Chill for at least 6 hours or overnight. Cut into 1/4 inch (6 mm) slices with serrated knife. Arrange, about 1 inch (2.5 cm) apart, on greased cookie sheets. Bake in 375°F (190°C) oven for about 10 minutes until golden. Let stand on cookie sheets for 5 minutes before removing to wire racks to cool. Makes about 52 cookies.

1 cookie: 106 Calories; 6.3 g Total Fat (2.5 g Mono, 0.2 g Poly, 3.0 g Sat); 14 mg Cholesterol; 12 g Carbohydrate; trace Fibre; 1 g Protein; 59 mg Sodium

Fig and Poppy Florentines

These lacy confections are chewy with occasional bits of hazelnut and fig.
Store them in an airtight container at room temperature for up to three days,
or in the freezer for up to two months. If making these ahead, freeze the
cookies before dipping in chocolate.

Granulated sugar	3/4 cup	175 mL
Butter (or hard margarine)	1/4 cup	60 mL
Half-and-half cream	3 tbsp.	50 mL
Liquid honey	2 tbsp.	30 mL
Flaked hazelnuts (filberts)	1 cup	250 mL
Finely chopped dried figs	1/2 cup	125 mL
All-purpose flour	1/4 cup	60 mL
Poppy seeds	2 tbsp.	30 mL
Grated orange zest	1 tsp.	5 mL
Salt	1/8 tsp.	0.5 mL
Dark chocolate melting wafers	2/3 cup	150 mL

Combine first 4 ingredients in small saucepan on medium. Heat and stir for about 5 minutes until butter is melted and sugar is dissolved. Bring to a boil. Remove from heat.

Combine next 6 ingredients in small bowl. Add to sugar mixture. Stir well. Let stand for 30 minutes. Drop, using 2 tsp. (10 mL) for each, about 5 inches (12.5 cm) apart onto parchment paper-lined cookie sheets. Spread to 2 inch (5 cm) diameter with back of spoon. Bake in 350°F (175°C) oven for about 9 minutes until golden. Let stand on cookie sheets for 5 minutes before removing to wire racks to cool completely.

Place chocolate in small microwave-safe bowl. Microwave on medium, stirring every 30 seconds, until almost melted (see Tip, page 85). Stir until smooth. Dip one edge of each cookie into chocolate, allowing excess to drip back into bowl. Transfer to parchment paper-lined cookie sheets. Repeat with remaining cookies and chocolate. Let stand until set. Makes about 34 cookies.

1 cookie: 80 Calories; 4.4 g Total Fat (2.2 g Mono, 0.5 g Poly, 1.5 g Sat); 4 mg Cholesterol; 11 g Carbohydrate; 1 g Fibre; 1 g Protein; 19 mg Sodium

Pictured on page 126.

Orange Hazelnut Ganache Bites

The decadent chocolate flavour in these small squares is sure to satisfy.
Prepare and chill these bites a few hours before dinner, and present them
on a platter for dessert.

Whipping cream	2/3 cup	150 mL
Dark chocolate bars (3 1/2 oz., 100 g, each), chopped	7	7
Hazelnut liqueur	2 tbsp.	30 mL
Grated orange zest	1/2 tsp.	2 mL
Chopped flaked hazelnuts (filberts), toasted (see Tip, page 99)	1/4 cup	60 mL
Grated orange zest	1/4 tsp.	1 mL

Line 9 x 9 inch (23 x 23 cm) pan with greased foil, leaving 1 inch (2.5 cm) overhang on 2 sides. Set aside. Heat cream in medium saucepan on medium until very hot and bubbles form around edge of saucepan. Remove from heat.

Add next 3 ingredients. Stir until chocolate is melted. Pour into prepared pan.

Combine hazelnuts and second amount of orange zest in small bowl. Sprinkle over top. Chill for 2 to 3 hours until firm. Holding foil, remove chocolate mixture from pan. Cuts into 64 squares.

1 square: 72 Calories; 4.8 g Total Fat (0.5 g Mono, 0.1 g Poly, 2.9 g Sat); 4 mg Cholesterol; 7 g Carbohydrate; 1 g Fibre; 1 g Protein; 1 mg Sodium

Chocolate Peanut Bark

Divine chocolate and peanut flavours make this a treat worth wrapping up
for gifts. This crowd-pleasing and addictive snack can be made ahead.

Dark chocolate bars (3 1/2 oz., 100 g, each), chopped	4	4
Crisp rice cereal	1 cup	250 mL
Dry-roasted peanuts, coarsely chopped	1/4 cup	60 mL
Peanut butter chips	1/4 cup	60 mL

(continued on next page)

Candies & Cookies

Heat chocolate in medium heavy saucepan on lowest heat, stirring often, until almost melted. Remove from heat. Stir until smooth.

Add cereal. Stir until coated. Spread evenly on waxed paper-lined baking sheet with sides.

Scatter peanuts and peanut butter chips over top. Place waxed paper over top. Press down lightly. Chill for about 2 hours until firm. Break bark into irregular-shaped pieces. Makes about 40 pieces.

1 piece: 67 Calories; 4.0 g Total Fat (0.4 g Mono, 0.2 g Poly, 2.3 g Sat); 1 mg Cholesterol; 7 g Carbohydrate; 1 g Fibre; 1 g Protein; 9 mg Sodium

---

White Chocolate Ginger Fudge

A unique take on fudge, with ginger balancing the sweetness. This creamy sweet can be made ahead and served on a tray of goodies.

Miniature marshmallows	4 cups	1 L
Granulated sugar	1 1/2 cups	375 mL
Evaporated milk	3/4 cup	175 mL
Butter (or hard margarine)	1/4 cup	60 mL
Salt	1/4 tsp.	1 mL
White chocolate chips	3 cups	750 mL
Chopped walnuts, toasted (see Tip, page 99)	1/2 cup	125 mL
Minced crystallized ginger	1/2 cup	125 mL

Line 9 x 9 inch (23 x 23 cm) pan with greased foil, leaving 1 inch (2.5 cm) overhang on 2 sides. Set aside. Combine first 5 ingredients in large saucepan. Heat and stir on medium until boiling. Boil for 5 minutes, stirring constantly. Remove from heat.

Add chocolate. Stir until melted.

Add walnuts and ginger. Stir. Spread evenly in prepared pan. Let stand at room temperature until set. Holding foil, remove fudge from pan. Cuts into 64 squares.

1 square: 89 Calories; 4.5 g Total Fat (0.3 g Mono, 0.5 g Poly, 2.4 g Sat); 6 mg Cholesterol; 13 g Carbohydrate; trace Fibre; 1 g Protein; 29 mg Sodium

Pictured on page 125.

Mince and Apple Rugelachs

These inviting rugelachs (pronounced RUHG-uh-luhkh), traditional Jewish pastries, have a comforting mincemeat and apple filling inside buttery pastry.

Butter (or hard margarine), softened	1 cup	250 mL
Block cream cheese, softened	8 oz.	250 g
Brown sugar, packed	1/2 cup	125 mL
All-purpose flour	2 1/4 cups	550 mL
Salt	1/4 tsp.	1 mL
Mincemeat	1 cup	250 mL
Finely chopped dried apple	1/2 cup	125 mL
Fine dry bread crumbs	2 tbsp.	30 mL
Egg white (large), fork-beaten	1	1
Granulated sugar	1 tbsp.	15 mL

Beat first 3 ingredients in large bowl until light and fluffy.

Add flour and salt. Stir until soft dough forms. Divide into 3 portions. Shape into flattened discs. Wrap with plastic wrap. Chill for at least 1 hour until firm.

Combine next 3 ingredients in small bowl. Let 1 portion of dough stand at room temperature for 10 minutes. Discard plastic wrap. Roll out on lightly floured surface to 12 inch (30 cm) diameter circle. Spread about 1/3 of mincemeat mixture over dough, leaving 1/4 inch (6 mm) edge. Cut into 12 wedges. Roll up each wedge, starting from wide end. Press pointed end against roll to seal. Arrange rolls, point-side down, about 2 inches (5 cm) apart, on parchment paper-lined cookie sheets. Repeat with remaining dough and mincemeat mixture.

Brush with egg white. Sprinkle with granulated sugar. Bake in 350°F (175°C) oven for about 22 minutes until golden. Makes about 36 cookies.

1 cookie: 120 Calories; 7.3 g Total Fat (1.9 g Mono, 0.3 g Poly, 4.6 g Sat); 20 mg Cholesterol; 13 g Carbohydrate; trace Fibre; 1 g Protein; 101 mg Sodium

Pictured on page 126.

Chocolate Spice Cookies

These moist and appetizing crackle cookies are loaded with spices and molasses flavour. This recipe makes a big batch—perfect for cookie exchanges. Spare a couple to leave out for Santa with a glass of milk!

All-purpose flour	2 cups	500 mL
Cocoa, sifted if lumpy	2 tbsp.	30 mL
Ground cinnamon	1 tbsp.	15 mL
Ground ginger	1 1/2 tsp.	7 mL
Baking soda	1 tsp.	5 mL
Ground cloves	1/2 tsp.	2 mL
Salt	1/2 tsp.	2 mL
Brown sugar, packed	1 cup	250 mL
Butter (or hard margarine)	1/2 cup	125 mL
Fancy (mild) molasses	1/2 cup	125 mL
Semi-sweet chocolate chips	1/2 cup	125 mL
Large egg, fork-beaten	1	1
Granulated sugar	1/4 cup	60 mL

Combine first 7 ingredients in medium bowl.

Combine next 4 ingredients in medium saucepan on medium-low. Heat and stir until chocolate is almost melted. Remove from heat. Stir until smooth. Transfer to large bowl. Let stand for 5 minutes.

Add egg. Stir well. Add flour mixture. Stir until no dry flour remains. Chill, covered, for about 1 hour until firm. Roll into balls, using 1 tbsp. (15 mL) for each.

Put granulated sugar in small shallow dish. Roll balls in sugar until coated. Arrange, about 2 inches (5 cm) apart, on greased cookie sheets. Bake in 350°F (175°C) oven for about 9 minutes until puffed and cracked on top. Let stand on cookie sheets for 5 minutes before removing to wire racks to cool. Makes about 54 cookies.

1 cookie: 63 Calories; 2.3 g Total Fat (0.6 g Mono, 0.1 g Poly, 1.4 g Sat); 8 mg Cholesterol; 11 g Carbohydrate; trace Fibre; 1 g Protein; 60 mg Sodium

Gingerbread Biscotti

Dark, crisp biscotti with a classic gingerbread flavour. Serve these with Christmas tea or afternoon coffee. Biscotti are always beautiful when individually packaged as gifts.

All-purpose flour	2 cups	500 mL
Brown sugar, packed	1 cup	250 mL
Sliced natural almonds, chopped	1/2 cup	125 mL
Baking powder	1 tsp.	5 mL
Ground ginger	1 tsp.	5 mL
Ground cinnamon	3/4 tsp.	4 mL
Salt	1/2 tsp.	2 mL
Baking soda	1/4 tsp.	1 mL
Ground nutmeg	1/4 tsp.	1 mL
Large eggs, fork-beaten	2	2
Butter (or hard margarine), melted	1/3 cup	75 mL
Fancy (mild) molasses	1/4 cup	60 mL
Minced crystallized ginger	1/4 cup	60 mL

Combine first 9 ingredients in large bowl. Make a well in centre.

Combine remaining 4 ingredients in small bowl. Add to well. Mix until stiff dough forms. Turn out onto lightly floured surface. Knead 6 times. Divide into 2 portions. Shape into 8 inch (20 cm) long logs. Place crosswise, about 3 inches (7.5 cm) apart, on greased cookie sheet. Flatten slightly. Bake in 350°F (175°C) oven for 25 minutes. Let stand on cookie sheet for about 10 minutes until cool enough to handle. Transfer to cutting board. Cut logs diagonally into 1/2 inch (12 mm) slices with serrated knife. Arrange, cut-side-down, on greased cookie sheet. Bake for about 10 minutes per side until dry and crisp. Let stand on cookie sheet for 5 minutes before removing to wire rack to cool. Makes about 34 biscotti.

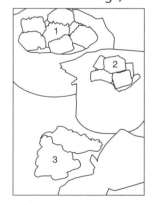

1 biscotti: 86 Calories; 2.8 g Total Fat (1.0 g Mono, 0.3 g Poly, 1.3 g Sat); 17 mg Cholesterol; 15 g Carbohydrate; trace Fibre; 1 g Protein; 78 mg Sodium

1. Toffee Truffle Brownies, page 138
2. White Chocolate Ginger Fudge, page 121
3. Christmas Tree Cookies, page 128

Props: Walmart

Fruit and Cashew Clusters

Toasted coconut coats these delicious white chocolate no-bake clusters that chill in the fridge until you're ready for them. They will store in an airtight container in the refrigerator for up to one month, or in the freezer for up to two months.

White chocolate bars (3 1/2 oz., 100 g, each), chopped	4	4
Chopped salted cashews	1 cup	250 mL
Finely chopped pitted dates	1/2 cup	125 mL
Golden raisins	1/2 cup	125 mL
Medium unsweetened coconut, toasted (see Tip, page 99)	1 1/4 cups	300 mL

Heat chocolate in medium heavy saucepan on lowest heat, stirring often, until chocolate is almost melted. Remove from heat. Stir until smooth.

Add next 3 ingredients. Stir well. Let stand at room temperature for 1 to 1 1/2 hours until cool enough to handle.

Place coconut in large shallow dish. Drop mounds of chocolate mixture, using 1 tbsp. (15 mL) for each, into coconut. Roll in coconut until coated. Arrange on waxed paper-lined baking sheet. Chill until firm. Makes about 48 clusters.

1 cluster: 90 Calories; 5.8 g Total Fat (0.1 g Mono, trace Poly, 3.2 g Sat); 2 mg Cholesterol; 9 g Carbohydrate; 1 g Fibre; 1 g Protein; 31 mg Sodium

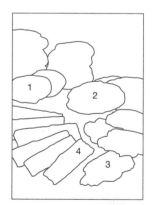

1. Cranberry Pistachio Cookies, page 130
2. Fig and Poppy Florentines, page 119
3. Mince and Apple Rugelachs, page 122
4. White Chocolate Panforte, page 117

Christmas Tree Cookies

If your favourite part of the holidays is trimming the tree, these are for you—sweet vanilla cookies speckled with cinnamon and "trimmed" with fun decorations. If making these ahead, freeze the cookies before icing and decorating.

Granulated sugar	3/4 cup	175 mL
Butter (or hard margarine), softened	1/2 cup	125 mL
Vegetable shortening, softened	1/2 cup	125 mL
Large eggs	2	2
Maple syrup	3 tbsp.	50 mL
Vanilla extract	1/2 tsp.	2 mL
All-purpose flour	3 cups	750 mL
Baking powder	1 1/2 tsp.	7 mL
Salt	1/4 tsp.	1 mL
Ground cinnamon	1/4 tsp.	1 mL
Icing (confectioner's) sugar	2 1/2 cups	625 mL
Pasteurized egg white product	2 tbsp.	30 mL
Water	2 tsp.	10 mL
Lemon juice	1 tsp.	5 mL
Drops of green liquid food colouring	6	6
Drops of yellow liquid food colouring	6	6
Mini candy-coated chocolates	1 cup	250 mL

Beat first 3 ingredients in large bowl until light and fluffy.

Add eggs, 1 at a time, beating well after each addition. Add maple syrup and vanilla. Beat well.

Combine next 4 ingredients in small bowl. Add to sugar mixture in 2 additions, mixing well after each addition until no dry flour remains. Divide into 2 portions. Shape into flattened discs. Wrap in plastic wrap. Chill for 1 hour. Let dough stand at room temperature for 10 minutes. Discard plastic wrap. Roll out dough on lightly floured surface to 1/4 inch (6 mm) thickness. Cut out shapes with lightly floured 4 inch (10 cm) tree-shaped cookie cutter. Roll out scraps to cut more shapes. Arrange about 1 inch (2.5 cm) apart on greased cookie sheets. Bake in 350°F (175°C) oven for about 14 minutes until golden. Let stand on cookie sheets for 5 minutes before removing to wire racks to cool completely.

(continued on next page)

Beat next 6 ingredients in medium bowl until stiff peaks form. Spoon into piping bag fitted with small writing tip (see Tip, page 131). Pipe onto 1 cookie.

Decorate with candy-coated chocolates. Let stand until set. Repeat with remaining cookies, icing and candy-coated chocolates. Makes about 36 cookies.

1 cookie: 158 Calories; 6.5 g Total Fat (1.8 g Mono, 0.8 g Poly, 3.0 g Sat); 19 mg Cholesterol; 23 g Carbohydrate; trace Fibre; 2 g Protein; 64 mg Sodium

Pictured on page 125.

Espresso Shortbread

Delectable grown-up tastes—the rich coffee flavours are highlighted by a chocolate-covered coffee bean. Savour one or two while you decorate the house, or use them as stocking stuffers for coffee lovers (if you feel like sharing)!

Butter, softened	1 cup	250 mL
Icing (confectioner's) sugar	2/3 cup	150 mL
Instant coffee granules, crushed to fine powder	1 tbsp.	15 mL
Ground cinnamon	1/4 tsp.	1 mL
All-purpose flour	2 cups	500 mL
Dark chocolate-covered coffee beans (or jumbo chocolate chips)	30	30

Beat first 4 ingredients in medium bowl until light and fluffy.

Add flour in 2 additions, mixing well after each addition, until no dry flour remains. Roll into balls, using 1 tbsp. (15 mL) for each. Arrange, about 1 inch (2.5 cm) apart, on ungreased cookie sheets. Flatten slightly with fork.

Press 1 coffee bean in centre of each cookie. Bake in 350°F (175°C) oven for about 12 minutes until bottoms are golden. Let stand on cookie sheets for 5 minutes before removing to wire racks to cool. Makes about 30 cookies.

1 cookie: 99 Calories; 6.5 g Total Fat (1.6 g Mono, 0.2 g Poly, 4.1 g Sat); 16 mg Cholesterol; 10 g Carbohydrate; trace Fibre; 1 g Protein; 43 mg Sodium

Pictured on page 18.

Cranberry Pistachio Cookies

Strikingly pretty butter cookies with colourful pistachios and cranberries. Set out a plate and watch these beauties vanish! This recipe makes lots, so keep some in your cookie jar and send some home with guests.

Butter, softened	1 cup	250 mL
Granulated sugar	1 cup	250 mL
Large egg	1	1
Egg yolk (large)	1	1
Grated orange zest	1 tbsp.	15 mL
Vanilla extract	1 tsp.	5 mL
All-purpose flour	2 1/2 cups	625 mL
Ground cinnamon	1/2 tsp.	2 mL
Ground allspice	1/4 tsp.	1 mL
Salt	1/4 tsp.	1 mL
Chopped dried cranberries	1 1/2 cups	375 mL
Chopped pistachios	1 1/2 cups	375 mL

Beat butter and sugar in large bowl until light and fluffy. Add next 4 ingredients. Beat well.

Combine next 4 ingredients in small bowl. Add to butter mixture in 2 additions, mixing well after each addition, until no dry flour remains.

Add cranberries and pistachios. Mix well. Divide into 2 portions. Roll into 9 inch (23 cm) long logs. Wrap with plastic wrap. Chill for at least 6 hours or overnight. Cut into 1/4 inch (6 mm) slices with serrated knife. Arrange, about 2 inches (5 cm) apart, on greased cookie sheets. Bake in 375°F (190°C) oven for about 10 minutes until golden. Let stand on cookie sheets for 5 minutes before removing to wire racks to cool. Makes about 64 cookies.

1 cookie: 76 Calories; 4.4 g Total Fat (1.5 g Mono, 0.6 g Poly, 2.0 g Sat); 14 mg Cholesterol; 9 g Carbohydrate; 1 g Fibre; 1 g Protein; 43 mg Sodium

Pictured on page 126.

Peppermint Mini-Cupcakes

You won't be able to eat just one! These mini-cupcakes are adorable, delicious and so festive, with a chocolate-covered mint candy hiding in each one.

Package of chocolate cake mix (1 layer size)	1	1
Small chocolate-covered soft peppermints (such as York Bites or Junior Mints)	36	36
Icing (confectioner's) sugar	3 cups	750 mL
Butter (or hard margarine), softened	3/4 cup	175 mL
Milk	3 tbsp.	50 mL
Peppermint extract	1/2 tsp.	2 mL
Crushed candy cane	2 tbsp.	30 mL

Prepare cake mix according to package directions. Fill 36 paper-lined mini-muffin cups 1/2 full.

Place 1 peppermint on each. Bake in 350°F (175°C) oven for about 12 minutes until wooden pick inserted in centre of cupcake comes out clean. Let stand in pan for 10 minutes before removing to wire rack to cool completely.

Beat next 4 ingredients on low in large bowl until combined. Beat on high for about 3 minutes until light and fluffy. Spoon into piping bag fitted with large star tip (see Tip, below). Pipe onto cupcakes.

Sprinkle with crushed candy before serving (see Note). Makes 36 mini-cupcakes.

1 mini-cupcake: 199 Calories; 8.8 g Total Fat (2.9 g Mono, 1.0 g Poly, 4.2 g Sat); 28 mg Cholesterol; 30 g Carbohydrate; 1 g Fibre; 2 g Protein; 128 mg Sodium

Pictured on page 143 and on back cover.

Note: These can be stored frozen and decorated in an airtight container for up to two months. Thaw uncovered at room temperature so that the candy cane sprinkle doesn't run. If you're making these cupcakes ahead and not freezing them, sprinkle with candy cane just before serving.

 tip If you don't have a piping bag, you can use a freezer bag with the corner snipped off.

Chocolate Toffee Crisps

Everyone's favourite flavours in a one-bite square—and easy to package up for gifts too! Freeze the remaining sweetened condensed milk for next time.

Butter (or hard margarine)	2 tbsp.	30 mL
Butterscotch toffee bars (2 oz., 56 g, each), or 16 bite-sized toffees (such as Mackintosh's)	2	2
Sweetened condensed milk	1/2 cup	125 mL
Crisp rice cereal	3 cups	750 mL
Slivered almonds, toasted (see Tip, page 99)	1/3 cup	75 mL
Toffee bits (such as Skor)	1/3 cup	75 mL
Semi-sweet chocolate chips	2/3 cup	150 mL
Butter (or hard margarine)	2 tbsp.	30 mL

Melt butter in large saucepan on medium. Add toffee and condensed milk. Heat and stir for about 4 minutes until smooth. Remove from heat.

Add next 3 ingredients. Stir until coated. Press firmly into greased 9 x 9 inch (23 x 23 cm) pan.

Heat chocolate chips and second amount of butter in small heavy saucepan on lowest heat, stirring often, until chocolate is almost melted. Remove from heat. Stir until smooth. Spread evenly over cereal mixture. Chill. Cuts into 36 squares.

1 square: 78 Calories; 4.0 g Total Fat (0.9 g Mono, 0.2 g Poly, 2.2 g Sat); 8 mg Cholesterol; 10 g Carbohydrate; trace Fibre; 1 g Protein; 61 mg Sodium

Golden Madeira Cake

A Christmas classic that's perfect to give, lovely to receive. This must chill for three days before serving, and can be stored in an airtight container in the refrigerator for up to one month.

Golden raisins	2 cups	500 mL
Chopped candied pineapple	1 cup	250 mL
Diced mixed peel	1 cup	250 mL
Madeira wine	1/2 cup	125 mL

(continued on next page)

Cakes & Squares

All-purpose flour	1 1/4 cups	300 mL
Chopped blanched almonds	1 cup	250 mL
Baking powder	1 tsp.	5 mL
Ground allspice	1/2 tsp.	2 mL
Salt	1/2 tsp.	2 mL
Butter (or hard margarine), softened	1/2 cup	125 mL
Granulated sugar	1/2 cup	125 mL
Large eggs, fork-beaten	2	2
Grated lemon zest	1 tbsp.	15 mL
Grated orange zest	1 tbsp.	15 mL
Almond extract	1 tsp.	5 mL
Whole blanched almonds	20	20
Candied pineapple slices	2	2
Madeira wine	1/4 cup	60 mL
Madeira wine	1/2 cup	125 mL

Combine first 4 ingredients in medium bowl. Let stand for 20 minutes.

Combine next 5 ingredients in separate medium bowl.

Beat butter and sugar in large bowl until light and fluffy. Add eggs, 1 at a time, beating well after each addition.

Add next 3 ingredients and flour mixture. Beat until smooth. Add fruit mixture. Stir well. Spread evenly in greased parchment paper-lined 9 x 5 x 3 inch (23 x 12.5 x 7.5 cm) loaf pan.

Arrange whole almonds and pineapple slices in decorative pattern over batter. Bake on centre rack in 300°F (150°C) oven for about 1 3/4 hours until wooden pick inserted in centre comes out clean. Remove from oven. Poke several holes randomly into cake with skewer.

Drizzle with of second amount of wine. Let stand in pan on wire rack until cooled completely. Remove cake from pan. Discard parchment paper.

Place 4 layers of cheesecloth in medium bowl. Pour third amount of wine over top. Let stand until wine is absorbed, adding more wine, if necessary, to soak cheesecloth. Wrap cake in cheesecloth. Wrap with plastic wrap. Wrap tightly with foil. Let stand in refrigerator for at least 3 days before serving. Cuts into 16 slices. Cut slices into 3 pieces each. Makes 48 pieces.

1 piece: 103 Calories; 3.4 g Total Fat (1.4 g Mono, 0.4 g Poly, 1.4 g Sat); 14 mg Cholesterol; 16 g Carbohydrate; 1 g Fibre; 1 g Protein; 61 mg Sodium

Holiday Gingerbread Bundt

This beautifully dark bundt cake is dusted with "snow" as a festive touch for get-togethers. Special ingredients like cocoa, applesauce and beer contribute to the deep flavours.

Stout (or dark) beer	1 cup	250 mL
Fancy (mild) molasses	2/3 cup	150 mL
Large eggs	3	3
Brown sugar, packed	1 cup	250 mL
Unsweetened applesauce	2/3 cup	150 mL
Cooking oil	1/2 cup	125 mL
All-purpose flour	2 1/2 cups	625 mL
Cocoa, sifted if lumpy	1/4 cup	60 mL
Ground ginger	2 tbsp.	30 mL
Baking powder	1 1/2 tsp.	7 mL
Baking soda	1 tsp.	5 mL
Ground cinnamon	1 tsp.	5 mL
Ground allspice	1/2 tsp.	2 mL
Ground nutmeg	1/2 tsp.	2 mL
Salt	1/2 tsp.	2 mL
Icing (confectioner's) sugar	1 tbsp.	15 mL

Combine beer and molasses in medium saucepan. Bring to a boil on medium. Carefully transfer to medium bowl. Let stand for about 1 hour, stirring occasionally, until cooled to room temperature.

Add next 4 ingredients. Beat until brown sugar is dissolved.

Combine next 9 ingredients in large bowl. Make a well in centre. Add beer mixture to well. Beat until smooth. Spread evenly in greased 12 cup (3 L) Bundt pan. Bake in 350°F (175°C) oven for about 45 minutes until wooden pick inserted in centre comes out clean. Let stand in pan on wire rack for 10 minutes. Invert onto wire rack to cool completely.

Dust with icing sugar. Cuts into 16 pieces.

1 piece: 242 Calories; 8.3 g Total Fat (4.6 g Mono, 2.3 g Poly, 0.9 g Sat); 40 mg Cholesterol; 40 g Carbohydrate; 1 g Fibre; 3 g Protein; 225 mg Sodium

Pictured on page 143 and on back cover.

Cakes & Squares

Mincemeat Brandy Squares

A traditional square that's great to keep on hand for those occasions when unexpected company drops by. Golden and coconut-topped, these squares are filled with soft mincemeat and a hint of brandy.

All-purpose flour	1 cup	250 mL
Brown sugar, packed	1 cup	250 mL
Finely crushed vanilla wafers (about 35 wafers)	1 cup	250 mL
Butter (or hard margarine), melted	3/4 cup	175 mL
Medium unsweetened coconut	1/2 cup	125 mL
Salt	1/2 tsp.	2 mL
Ground cinnamon	1/4 tsp.	1 mL
Large eggs	2	2
Brown sugar, packed	1 cup	250 mL
Brandy (or 1 tsp., 5 mL, brandy extract)	1 tbsp.	15 mL
All-purpose flour	1/3 cup	75 mL
Baking powder	1/2 tsp.	2 mL
Salt	1/4 tsp.	1 mL
Mincemeat	1 cup	250 mL

Combine first 7 ingredients in large bowl. Press 3 cups (750 mL) wafer crumb mixture firmly into greased 9 x 9 inch (23 x 23 cm) pan. Bake in 350°F (175°C) oven for 10 minutes.

Beat eggs in medium bowl until frothy. Add sugar and brandy. Stir.

Combine next 3 ingredients in small bowl. Add to egg mixture. Stir.

Add mincemeat. Stir well. Spread evenly over bottom layer. Sprinkle remaining wafer mixture over top. Bake for about 30 minutes until golden. Let stand in pan on wire rack until cool. Cuts into 36 squares.

1 square: 119 Calories; 5.1 g Total Fat (1.3 g Mono, 0.3 g Poly, 3.2 g Sat); 23 mg Cholesterol; 18 g Carbohydrate; trace Fibre; 1 g Protein; 105 mg Sodium

Cranberry Date Streusel Bars

Cool streusel bars with a chewy-sweet filling, a buttery streusel topping and a pecan crunch. These pleasant, attractive squares are made ahead and chilled.

Chopped pitted dates	2 cups	500 mL
Water	1 1/2 cups	375 mL
Dried cranberries	2 cups	500 mL
Grated orange zest	2 tsp.	10 mL
All-purpose flour	1 cup	250 mL
Brown sugar, packed	1 cup	250 mL
Baking soda	1/2 tsp.	2 mL
Salt	1/2 tsp.	2 mL
Cold butter (or hard margarine), cut up	1 cup	250 mL
Quick-cooking rolled oats	1 1/2 cups	375 mL
Chopped pecans, toasted (see Tip, page 99)	1/2 cup	125 mL

Place dates and water in medium saucepan. Bring to a boil. Reduce heat to medium-low. Simmer, uncovered, for 5 minutes, stirring occasionally.

Add cranberries and orange zest. Stir. Cool.

Combine next 4 ingredients in large bowl. Cut in butter until mixture resembles coarse crumbs.

Add oats and pecans. Mix well. Press 4 cups (1 L) firmly into greased 9 x 13 inch (23 x 33 cm) pan. Spread date mixture evenly over bottom layer. Sprinkle remaining oat mixture over top. Press down lightly. Bake in 375°F (190°C) oven for about 25 minutes until golden brown. Let stand in pan on wire rack until cool. Chill, covered, for at least 6 hours or overnight. Cuts into 32 bars.

1 bar: 167 Calories; 7.3 g Total Fat (2.2 g Mono, 0.6 g Poly, 3.7 g Sat); 15 mg Cholesterol; 26 g Carbohydrate; 2 g Fibre; 1 g Protein; 96 mg Sodium

Pecan Pie Squares

Enjoy all the flavour of classic pecan pie in a handheld square—these are rich and tasty with a shortbread crust.

All-purpose flour	1 cup	250 mL
Finely chopped pecans	1/2 cup	125 mL
Brown sugar, packed	2 tbsp.	30 mL
Cold butter (or hard margarine), cut up	1/2 cup	125 mL
Large egg	1	1
Corn syrup	1/2 cup	125 mL
Brown sugar, packed	1/4 cup	60 mL
All-purpose flour	2 tbsp.	30 mL
Butter (or hard margarine), melted	1 tbsp.	15 mL
Vanilla extract	1 tsp.	5 mL
Salt	1/4 tsp.	1 mL
Chopped pecans	1 cup	250 mL

Combine first 3 ingredients in medium bowl. Cut in butter until mixture resembles coarse crumbs. Press firmly into greased 9 x 9 inch (23 x 23 cm) pan. Bake in 350°F (175°C) oven for 15 minutes.

Beat egg in small bowl until frothy. Add next 6 ingredients. Beat until smooth.

Add second amount of pecans. Stir. Spread evenly over butter mixture. Bake in 350°F (175°C) oven for about 20 minutes until filling is golden and set. Let stand in pan on wire rack until cool. Cuts into 36 squares.

1 square: 95 Calories; 6.6 g Total Fat (2.8 g Mono, 1.2 g Poly, 2.2 g Sat); 13 mg Cholesterol; 9 g Carbohydrate; 1 g Fibre; 1 g Protein; 41 mg Sodium

Paré Pointer

The pig joined the army because he heard the food was a mess.

Toffee Truffle Brownies

Tempting brownie bites that taste more decadent than they actually are—so you can indulge a sweet tooth without going overboard! To make these ahead, freeze the brownies before icing and decorating.

Semi-sweet chocolate baking squares (1 oz., 28 g, each), coarsely chopped	2	2
Granulated sugar	1 cup	250 mL
All-purpose flour	3/4 cup	175 mL
Cocoa, sifted if lumpy	1/2 cup	125 mL
Salt	1/4 tsp.	1 mL
Egg whites (large)	2	2
Large egg	1	1
Unsweetened applesauce	1/2 cup	125 mL
Cooking oil	3 tbsp.	50 mL
Vanilla extract	1 tsp.	5 mL
White chocolate baking squares (1 oz., 28 g, each), coarsely chopped	3	3
Toffee bits (such as Skor)	1/2 cup	125 mL

Put semi-sweet chocolate into small microwave-safe bowl. Microwave on medium, stirring every 30 seconds, until almost melted (see Tip, page 85). Stir until smooth.

Combine next 4 ingredients in medium bowl. Make a well in centre.

Beat next 5 ingredients in small bowl. Add semi-sweet chocolate. Beat until smooth. Add to well. Stir until just combined. Spread in greased 9 x 9 inch (23 x 23 cm) pan. Bake in 350°F (175°C) oven for about 23 minutes until wooden pick inserted in centre of brownie comes out moist but not wet with batter. Do not overbake. Let stand in pan on wire rack until cool.

Put white chocolate into small microwave-safe bowl. Microwave on medium, stirring every 30 seconds, until almost melted. Stir until smooth. Spread over brownies.

Sprinkle with toffee bits. Let stand until set. Cuts into 36 squares.

1 square: 75 Calories; 3.6 g Total Fat (0.9 g Mono, 0.4 g Poly, 1.4 g Sat); 9 mg Cholesterol; 11 g Carbohydrate; 1 g Fibre; 1 g Protein; 37 mg Sodium

Pictured on page 125.

Christmas Fruit 'n' Nut Bars

These glossy squares include a nice variety of fruit, seeds and nuts which add great texture. You can also wrap them individually and give them as gifts.

Butter (or hard margarine)	1/3 cup	75 mL
Liquid honey	1/2 cup	125 mL
Brown sugar, packed	1/4 cup	60 mL
Ground cinnamon	1/2 tsp.	2 mL
Chopped walnuts, toasted (see Tip, page 99)	1 cup	250 mL
Chopped dried cherries	1/2 cup	125 mL
Chopped dark raisins	1/4 cup	60 mL
Finely chopped dried pineapple	1/4 cup	60 mL
Raw pumpkin seeds	1/4 cup	60 mL
Salted, roasted sunflower seeds	1/4 cup	60 mL
Minced crystallized ginger	3 tbsp.	50 mL
Cornflakes cereal	1 3/4 cups	425 mL
Quick-cooking rolled oats	1 1/4 cups	300 mL

Melt butter in large saucepan on medium. Add next 3 ingredients. Heat and stir until boiling. Boil for 1 minute. Remove from heat.

Add next 7 ingredients. Stir well.

Add cereal and rolled oats. Stir until coated. Press firmly into greased 9 x 9 inch (23 x 23 cm) pan. Let stand in pan on wire rack until cool. Cuts into 24 bars.

1 bar: 150 Calories; 7.5 g Total Fat (1.1 g Mono, 2.5 g Poly, 2.1 g Sat); 7 mg Cholesterol; 20 g Carbohydrate; 1 g Fibre; 2 g Protein; 35 mg Sodium

---

Paré Pointer

She plays the piano by ear. Her father fiddles with his whiskers.

Orange Chocolate Pie

A light and airy pie to please any sweet tooth! Fresh orange flavour accents a smooth chocolate mousse filling.

Butter (or hard margarine)	1/3 cup	75 mL
Chocolate wafer crumbs	1 1/2 cups	375 mL
Icing (confectioner's) sugar	2 tbsp.	30 mL
Skim milk powder	1/2 cup	125 mL
Granulated sugar	1/4 cup	60 mL
Butter (or hard margarine), softened	2 tbsp.	30 mL
Water	2 tbsp.	30 mL
Block cream cheese, softened	8 oz.	250 g
Granulated sugar	1/4 cup	60 mL
Frozen concentrated orange juice, thawed	1/2 cup	125 mL
Grated orange zest	1 tbsp.	15 mL
Envelope of dessert topping (not prepared)	1	1
Milk	1/2 cup	125 mL
Chocolate milk powder	1/4 cup	60 mL

Melt first amount of butter in small saucepan. Remove from heat. Add wafer crumbs and icing sugar. Stir until well mixed. Reserve 2 tbsp. (30 mL) crumb mixture in small bowl. Press remaining crumb mixture firmly in bottom and up sides of ungreased 9 inch (23 cm) pie plate. Bake in 350°F (175°C) oven for 10 minutes. Cool.

Beat next 4 ingredients in large bowl until combined.

Add cream cheese and second amount of granulated sugar. Beat until smooth.

Add concentrated orange juice and zest. Beat well.

Beat remaining 3 ingredients with same beaters in medium bowl until smooth and thickened. Fold into cream cheese mixture. Spread evenly in pie shell. Sprinkle with reserved crumb mixture. Chill for at least 3 hours until set. Cuts into 12 wedges.

1 wedge: 291 Calories; 15.8 g Total Fat (4.4 g Mono, 1.1 g Poly, 9.4 g Sat); 40 mg Cholesterol; 32 g Carbohydrate; 1 g Fibre; 7 g Protein; 256 mg Sodium

Mocha Tiramisu Trifle

An attractive variation of tiramisu that shows off chocolatey mocha layers.
Tangy yogurt replaces the traditional cheese for a smarter version of this
tempting dessert. This is best served the day it's made.

Box of instant chocolate pudding powder (6-serving size)	1	1
Milk	1 cup	250 mL
Chocolate liqueur	1/4 cup	60 mL
Coffee (or vanilla) yogurt	4 cups	1 L
Cold strong prepared coffee	1 1/2 cups	375 mL
Chocolate liqueur	3 tbsp.	50 mL
Ladyfingers, halved crosswise	15	15
Frozen whipped topping, thawed	3 cups	750 mL
Cocoa, sifted if lumpy	2 tsp.	10 mL
Ladyfingers, halved crosswise	20	20
Cocoa, sifted if lumpy	2 tsp.	10 mL

Beat first 3 ingredients in medium bowl until smooth. Add yogurt. Mix well.

Combine coffee and second amount of liqueur in small shallow dish.

Dip first amount of ladyfingers, 1 at a time, into coffee mixture. Arrange, cut-side down, around inside edge of 14 cup (3.5 L) trifle bowl or deep glass serving bowl. Arrange single layer of ladyfingers to cover bottom of bowl, trimming to fit if necessary. Spread half of yogurt mixture over ladyfingers.

Spread half of whipped topping over yogurt mixture. Dust with first amount of cocoa.

Dip second amount of ladyfingers, 1 at a time, into remaining coffee mixture. Arrange, cut-side down, around inside edge of trifle bowl. Arrange double layer of ladyfingers to cover cocoa. Spread remaining yogurt mixture over ladyfingers. Spread remaining whipped topping over yogurt mixture. Dust with second amount of cocoa. Chill, covered, for 4 hours. Makes about 14 cups (3.5 L).

1 cup (250 mL): 287 Calories; 10.8 g Total Fat (1.5 g Mono, 0.5 g Poly, 7.3 g Sat);
105 mg Cholesterol; 42 g Carbohydrate; 1 g Fibre; 8 g Protein; 164 mg Sodium

Pictured on page 144.

Tea-Spiced Poached Pears

*These subtly spiced pears are brightened with a sweet syrup drizzle. A light,
not-too-sweet option to finish off those large feasts with the family.*

Water	3 cups	750 mL
Granulated sugar	1/2 cup	125 mL
Cinnamon sticks (4 inches, 10 cm, each)	2	2
Whole black peppercorns	1/2 tsp.	2 mL
Whole cloves	4	4
Medium peeled firm pears, halved and cores removed	4	4
Orange pekoe tea bags	2	2
Lemon juice	2 tsp.	10 mL

Combine first 5 ingredients in large saucepan. Bring to a boil.

Add pears and tea bags. Reduce heat to medium. Boil gently, uncovered,
for about 10 minutes until pears are almost tender. Remove from heat.
Remove and discard tea bags. Let stand, uncovered, for about 20 minutes
until pears are tender. Transfer pears with slotted spoon to cutting board.
Remove and discard cinnamon, cloves and peppercorns. Bring cooking
liquid to a boil on medium. Boil gently for about 20 minutes until reduced
to about 1 cup (250 mL).

Add lemon juice. Stir. Cut pear halves into thin slices, leaving top intact.
Fan pears halves on 4 serving plates. Drizzle with tea mixture. Serves 4.

*1 serving: 161 Calories; 1.0 g Total Fat (0 g Mono, 0 g Poly, 0 g Sat); 0 mg Cholesterol;
43 g Carbohydrate; 4 g Fibre; 1 g Protein; trace Sodium*

1. Holiday Gingerbread Bundt, page 134
2. Peppermint Mini-Cupcakes, page 131

Props: HomeSense

Frozen Cheesecake Bars

This frozen dessert can be made ahead and stored in the freezer until serving time. A beautiful glaze is marbled into the surface of this fluffy pink cheesecake.

Butter (or hard margarine)	1/4 cup	60 mL
Chocolate wafer crumbs	1 1/4 cups	300 mL
Brown sugar, packed	1/4 cup	60 mL
Can of sweetened condensed milk	11 oz.	300 mL
Tub of strawberry cream cheese	8 oz.	250 g
Frozen whipped topping, thawed	1 cup	250 mL
Strawberry ice cream topping	1/2 cup	125 mL

Melt butter in small saucepan. Remove from heat. Add wafer crumbs and brown sugar. Stir until well mixed. Press firmly into ungreased 9 x 9 inch (23 x 23 cm) pan.

Beat condensed milk and cream cheese in large bowl until combined.

Fold in whipped topping. Spread evenly over crust.

Drizzle with ice cream topping. Drag wooden pick through topping to create decorative pattern. Freeze for about 4 hours until firm. Cuts into 16 squares.

1 square: 228 Calories; 10.9 g Total Fat (1.2 g Mono, 0.5 g Poly, 6.6 g Sat); 25 mg Cholesterol; 31 g Carbohydrate; trace Fibre; 3 g Protein; 146 mg Sodium

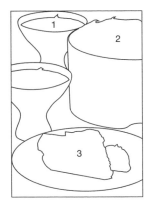

1. Raspberry Pomegranate Mousse, page 148
2. Mocha Tiramisu Trifle, page 141
3. Phyllo Apple Pie, page 150

Black Forest Pudding

A cake-like steamed pudding rich with chocolate and bits of sour cherry, paired with a delightfully tart sauce and a whipped cream garnish. Serve it warm or chilled.

All-purpose flour	1 1/3 cups	325 mL
Cocoa, sifted if lumpy	3 tbsp.	50 mL
Baking powder	1 tbsp.	15 mL
Salt	1/2 tsp.	2 mL
Butter (or hard margarine), softened	1/4 cup	60 mL
Granulated sugar	1/2 cup	125 mL
Large egg	1	1
Vanilla extract	1/2 tsp.	2 mL
Jar of pitted sour cherries in light syrup, drained and syrup reserved	16.9 oz.	500 mL
Milk	2/3 cup	150 mL
SAUCE		
Reserved cherry syrup	1 cup	250 mL
Granulated sugar	2 tbsp.	30 mL
Brandy (optional)	1 tbsp.	15 mL
Cornstarch	2 tsp.	10 mL
Whipping cream, whipped	1/2 cup	125 mL

Combine first 4 ingredients in small bowl.

Beat butter and sugar in medium bowl until light and fluffy. Add egg and vanilla. Beat well.

Add cherries. Stir.

Add flour mixture in 3 additions, alternating with milk in 2 additions, stirring well after each addition, until just combined. Spread evenly in well-greased 6 cup (1.5 L) heatproof bowl. Bowl should be about 2/3 full. Cover with greased foil. Place on wire rack set in medium roasting pan. Carefully pour boiling water into pan until water comes halfway up side of bowl. Bake in 350°F (175°C) oven for about 1 hour 15 minutes until wooden pick inserted in centre comes out clean. Carefully remove bowl from water. Let stand for 5 minutes before inverting onto wire rack to cool. Cuts into 8 wedges.

(continued on next page)

Desserts

Sauce: Stir first 4 ingredients in small saucepan until smooth. Bring to a boil on medium. Heat and stir for about 1 minute until thickened. Serve with pudding.

Garnish individual servings with whipped cream. Serves 8.

1 serving: 304 Calories; 12.4 g Total Fat (3.5 g Mono, 0.5 g Poly, 7.5 g Sat); 63 mg Cholesterol; 48 g Carbohydrate; 2 g Fibre; 5 g Protein; 422 mg Sodium

Baked Rice Pudding

This gently spiced rice pudding is studded with apricots and raisins and is great for potlucks, as it transports easily in one dish.

Milk	2 cups	500 mL
Salt	1/2 tsp.	2 mL
Long-grain white rice	1 cup	250 mL
Large eggs	2	2
Can of coconut milk	14 oz.	398 mL
Brown sugar, packed	1/4 cup	60 mL
Ground cinnamon	1/2 tsp.	2 mL
Vanilla extract	1/2 tsp.	2 mL
Ground nutmeg	1/4 tsp.	1 mL
Chopped dried apricot	1 cup	250 mL
Golden raisins	1/2 cup	125 mL

Combine milk and salt in medium saucepan. Bring to a boil. Add rice. Stir. Reduce heat to medium-low. Simmer, covered, for 15 minutes, without stirring. Remove from heat. Let stand, covered, for about 5 minutes until rice is tender and liquid is absorbed. Fluff with fork.

Beat eggs and coconut milk in large bowl until frothy. Add next 4 ingredients. Beat until smooth.

Add apricot, raisins and rice. Stir well. Spread evenly in greased 2 quart (2 L) shallow baking dish. Place baking dish in large roasting pan. Carefully pour boiling water into pan until halfway up side of baking dish. Bake in 350°F (175°C) oven for about 45 minutes until edges are golden and knife inserted in centre of pudding comes out clean. Makes about 5 cups (1.25 L).

1 cup (250 mL): 535 Calories; 20.3 g Total Fat (2.0 g Mono, 0.6 g Poly, 16.4 g Sat); 91 mg Cholesterol; 80 g Carbohydrate; 4 g Fibre; 12 g Protein; 346 mg Sodium

Raspberry Pomegranate Mousse

Pretty pink mousse cups make a light ending to a meal—and your guests will never guess that these have a healthful boost from tofu.

Packages of plain dessert tofu (10.7 oz., 300 g, each)	2	2
Frozen whole raspberries	2 cups	500 mL
Pomegranate juice	1/4 cup	60 mL
Vanilla extract	1/2 tsp.	2 mL
Egg whites (large), room temperature (see Safety Tip)	2	2
Salt, just a pinch		
Granulated sugar	3 tbsp.	50 mL
Frozen whole raspberries, thawed, for garnish		

Process first 4 ingredients in blender or food processor until smooth.

Beat egg whites in large bowl until frothy. Add salt. Beat until soft peaks form.

Add sugar, 1 tbsp. (15 mL) at a time, beating constantly until stiff peaks form. Slowly fold in tofu mixture until combined. Spoon into 6 parfait glasses. Chill for 2 to 3 hours until set.

Garnish with second amount of raspberries. Serve immediately. Serves 6.

1 serving: 114 Calories; 2.0 g Total Fat (0.4 g Mono, 1.1 g Poly, 0.3 g Sat); 0 mg Cholesterol; 15 g Carbohydrate; 1 g Fibre; 9 g Protein; 84 mg Sodium

Pictured on page 144.

Safety Tip: This recipe contains uncooked egg. Make sure to use fresh, clean Grade A eggs that are free of cracks. Keep chilled until consumed. Pregnant women, young children and the elderly are not advised to eat anything containing raw egg.

Fruity Rice Pudding

This rice pudding is festively topped with toasted almonds and cranberries for a delicious change from the ordinary. Sure to have guests coming back for seconds.

Water	2 cups	500 mL
Ground cinnamon	1/2 tsp.	2 mL
Salt	1/4 tsp.	1 mL
Long-grain brown rice	1 cup	250 mL
Boxes of instant vanilla pudding powder (4-serving size)	2	2
Milk	3 cups	750 mL
Cans of fruit cocktail (14 oz., 398 mL, each), drained	2	2
Grated orange zest	1 tsp.	5 mL
Frozen whipped topping, thawed	1 cup	250 mL
Dried cranberries	1/2 cup	125 mL
Slivered almonds, toasted (see Tip, page 99)	1/2 cup	125 mL

Combine first 3 ingredients in medium saucepan. Bring to a boil. Add rice. Stir. Reduce heat to medium-low. Simmer, covered, for about 35 minutes, without stirring, until rice is tender. Remove from heat. Let stand, covered, for about 5 minutes until liquid is absorbed. Fluff with fork. Cool.

Beat pudding powder and milk in large bowl for about 2 minutes until starting to thicken. Add rice. Stir well. Chill for about 3 hours until cold.

Add fruit cocktail and orange zest. Stir. Fold in whipped topping.

Scatter cranberries and almonds over top. Makes about 8 cups (2 L).

1 cup (250 mL): 367 Calories; 7.3 g Total Fat (2.8 g Mono, 1.2 g Poly, 3.0 g Sat); 6 mg Cholesterol; 72 g Carbohydrate; 4 g Fibre; 7 g Protein; 302 mg Sodium

Paré Pointer

Several frogs sitting on top of each other are a toad-em pole.

Phyllo Apple Pie

Tender couscous makes for a pleasantly textured filling, while apples and spices provide a classic apple pie flavour. The gorgeous golden phyllo crust is sprinkled with cinnamon sugar.

Apple juice	1 cup	250 mL
Ground cinnamon	1/4 tsp.	1 mL
Salt	1/8 tsp.	0.5 mL
Ground cloves, just a pinch		
Plain couscous	1/2 cup	125 mL
Can of apple pie filling	19 oz.	540 mL
Dark raisins	1/2 cup	125 mL
Crushed gingersnaps (about 5 gingersnaps)	1/4 cup	60 mL
Phyllo pastry sheets, thawed according to package directions	5	5
Cooking spray		
Crushed gingersnaps (about 2 gingersnaps)	2 tbsp.	30 mL
Granulated sugar	4 tsp.	20 mL
Ground cinnamon	1/8 tsp.	0.5 mL

Combine first 4 ingredients in small saucepan. Bring to a boil. Add couscous. Stir. Remove from heat. Let stand, covered, for 5 minutes. Fluff with fork. Cool.

Combine next 3 ingredients in small bowl.

Place 1 pastry sheet on work surface. Cover remaining sheets with damp towel to prevent drying. Spray pastry sheet with cooking spray. Sprinkle with 1 tsp. (5 mL) of second amount of gingersnap. Fold into thirds lengthwise to make 4 inch (10 cm) strip. Repeat with remaining cooking spray, pastry sheets and gingersnaps. Place 1 pastry sheet in greased 9 inch (23 cm) pie plate, allowing strip to hang over edge. Place second sheet over first, at an angle and slightly overlapping. Repeat with remaining pastry sheets until entire pie plate is covered (see Diagram 1). Gently press pastry to fit in pan, forming crust. Spray with cooking spray. Press couscous mixture firmly into bottom of crust. Spread pie filling mixture over couscous (see Diagram 2). Fold overhanging pastry over filling toward centre of pie. Spray with cooking spray.

(continued on next page)

Desserts

Stir sugar and second amount of cinnamon in small cup. Sprinkle over top. Bake on bottom rack in 350°F (175°C) oven for about 45 minutes until pastry is crisp and golden. Let stand for 15 minutes. Cuts into 8 wedges.

1 wedge: 222 Calories; 1.6 g Total Fat (0.7 g Mono, 0.2 g Poly, 0.4 g Sat); 0 mg Cholesterol; 50 g Carbohydrate; 2 g Fibre; 3 g Protein; 168 mg Sodium

Pictured on page 144.

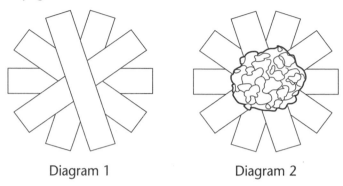

Diagram 1   Diagram 2

Chocolate Mole Fondue

This thick and delicious fondue was inspired by the Mexican flavours of mole (pronounced MOH-lay), made famous for its combination of chocolate and chilies. The sauce keeps its texture as it cools, so a fancy fondue pot is not required. Serve with wedges of apple or pear, strawberries and vanilla wafers.

Miniature marshmallows	2 cups	500 mL
Half-and-half cream	1/2 cup	125 mL
Instant coffee granules	1 tsp.	5 mL
Ground cinnamon	1/4 tsp.	1 mL
Cayenne pepper	1/8 tsp.	0.5 mL
Bittersweet chocolate baking squares (1 oz., 28 g, each), chopped	4	4

Combine first 5 ingredients in small saucepan on medium-low. Cook for about 15 minutes, stirring occasionally, until marshmallows are melted. Remove from heat.

Add chocolate. Stir until smooth. Carefully pour into fondue pot. Place over low heat. Makes about 1 1/3 cups (325 mL).

1/4 cup (60 mL): 176 Calories; 5.8 g Total Fat (1.8 g Mono, 0.4 g Poly, 3.4 g Sat); 8 mg Cholesterol; 32 g Carbohydrate; 1 g Fibre; 2 g Protein; 24 mg Sodium

Frozen Coconut Lime Torte

Refreshing flavours to bring a touch of the tropics to your celebration.
This torte can be stored in an airtight container in the freezer for up to one
month—let it stand at room temperature for ten minutes before slicing.

Butter (or hard margarine)	1/2 cup	125 mL
Finely crushed vanilla wafers (about 60 wafers)	1 3/4 cups	425 mL
Medium sweetened coconut, toasted (see Tip, page 99)	2/3 cup	150 mL
Can of sweetened condensed milk	11 oz.	300 mL
Lime juice	1/2 cup	125 mL
Grated lime zest (see Tip, below)	1 1/2 tsp.	7 mL
Coconut extract	1 tsp.	5 mL
Whipping cream	2 cups	500 mL
Medium sweetened coconut, toasted (see Tip, page 99)	1 cup	250 mL

Melt butter in medium saucepan. Remove from heat. Add wafer crumbs
and coconut. Stir until well mixed. Press firmly in bottom and 1 inch (2.5 cm)
up sides of greased 9 inch (23 cm) springform pan. Chill for 1 hour.

Beat next 4 ingredients in small bowl until smooth and thickened.

Beat whipping cream with same beaters in large bowl until stiff peaks form.
Fold in condensed milk mixture and coconut. Spread evenly over crust.
Freeze for at least 6 hours or overnight until firm. Cuts into 12 wedges.

1 wedge: 396 Calories; 29.4 g Total Fat (7.1 g Mono, 1.3 g Poly, 18.7 g Sat); 87 mg Cholesterol;
30 g Carbohydrate; 1 g Fibre; 4 g Protein; 148 mg Sodium

 When a recipe calls for grated zest and juice, it's easier to grate
the fruit first, then juice it. Be careful not to grate down to the
pith (white part of the peel), which is bitter and best avoided.

Measurement Tables

Throughout this book measurements are given in Conventional and Metric measure. To compensate for differences between the two measurements due to rounding, a full metric measure is not always used. The cup used is the standard 8 fluid ounce. Temperature is given in degrees Fahrenheit and Celsius. Baking pan measurements are in inches and centimetres as well as quarts and litres. An exact metric conversion is given below as well as the working equivalent (Metric Standard Measure).

Spoons

Conventional Measure	Metric Exact Conversion Millilitre (mL)	Metric Standard Measure Millilitre (mL)
1/8 teaspoon (tsp.)	0.6 mL	0.5 mL
1/4 teaspoon (tsp.)	1.2 mL	1 mL
1/2 teaspoon (tsp.)	2.4 mL	2 mL
1 teaspoon (tsp.)	4.7 mL	5 mL
2 teaspoons (tsp.)	9.4 mL	10 mL
1 tablespoon (tbsp.)	14.2 mL	15 mL

Cups

Conventional Measure	Metric Exact Conversion Millilitre (mL)	Metric Standard Measure Millilitre (mL)
1/4 cup (4 tbsp.)	56.8 mL	60 mL
1/3 cup (5 1/3 tbsp.)	75.6 mL	75 mL
1/2 cup (8 tbsp.)	113.7 mL	125 mL
2/3 cup (10 2/3 tbsp.)	151.2 mL	150 mL
3/4 cup (12 tbsp.)	170.5 mL	175 mL
1 cup (16 tbsp.)	227.3 mL	250 mL
4 1/2 cups	1022.9 mL	1000 mL (1 L)

Oven Temperatures

Fahrenheit (°F)	Celsius (°C)
175°	80°
200°	95°
225°	110°
250°	120°
275°	140°
300°	150°
325°	160°
350°	175°
375°	190°
400°	205°
425°	220°
450°	230°
475°	240°
500°	260°

Dry Measurements

Conventional Measure Ounces (oz.)	Metric Exact Conversion Grams (g)	Metric Standard Measure Grams (g)
1 oz.	28.3 g	28 g
2 oz.	56.7 g	57 g
3 oz.	85.0 g	85 g
4 oz.	113.4 g	125 g
5 oz.	141.7 g	140 g
6 oz.	170.1 g	170 g
7 oz.	198.4 g	200 g
8 oz.	226.8 g	250 g
16 oz.	453.6 g	500 g
32 oz.	907.2 g	1000 g (1 kg)

Pans

Conventional Inches	Metric Centimetres
8x8 inch	20x20 cm
9x9 inch	22x22 cm
9x13 inch	22x33 cm
10x15 inch	25x38 cm
11x17 inch	28x43 cm
8x2 inch round	20x5 cm
9x2 inch round	22x5 cm
10x4 1/2 inch tube	25x11 cm
8x4x3 inch loaf	20x10x7.5 cm
9x5x3 inch loaf	22x12.5x7.5 cm

Casseroles

CANADA & BRITAIN Standard Size Casserole	Exact Metric Measure	UNITED STATES Standard Size Casserole	Exact Metric Measure
1 qt. (5 cups)	1.13 L	1 qt. (4 cups)	900 mL
1 1/2 qts. (7 1/2 cups)	1.69 L	1 1/2 qts. (6 cups)	1.35 L
2 qts. (10 cups)	2.25 L	2 qts. (8 cups)	1.8 L
2 1/2 qts. (12 1/2 cups)	2.81 L	2 1/2 qts. (10 cups)	2.25 L
3 qts. (15 cups)	3.38 L	3 qts. (12 cups)	2.7 L
4 qts. (20 cups)	4.5 L	4 qts. (16 cups)	3.6 L
5 qts. (25 cups)	5.63 L	5 qts. (20 cups)	4.5 L

Recipe Index

155

156

157

Q

R

S

158

159

If you like what we've done with **cooking,** you'll **love** what we do with **crafts**!